LAW IN PRACTICE

■ ■ ■

by

Prentiss Cox
Associate Professor of Law
University of Minnesota Law School

Laura Thomas
Associate Professor of Clinical Instruction
University of Minnesota Law School

AMERICAN CASEBOOK SERIES®

WEST
ACADEMIC
PUBLISHING

Mat #41551208

American Casebook Series is a trademark registered in the U.S. Patent and Trademark Office.

© 2014 LEG, Inc. d/b/a West Academic
      444 Cedar Street, Suite 700
      St. Paul, MN 55101
      1-800-313-9378

West, West Academic Publishing, and West Academic are trademarks of West Publishing Corporation, used under license.

Printed in the United States of America

ISBN: 978–0–314–29077–9

Dedicated to Bess, Devon and Hallie—all so different and all loved alike

P.C.

For Dr. Steven H. Hatting, a dedicated and inspiring teacher

L.T.

PREFACE

This e-textbook is intended for use in the Law in Practice course—a course that includes extensive simulated case files and videos of attorneys modeling skills needed to complete the simulations. Law in Practice is a survey course designed to introduce the complex and uncertain process of applying legal doctrine to help clients resolve disputes and create value in transactions or business planning. The course presents methods of thinking and skills that form the foundation of the legal profession.

Student engagement is the heart of Law in Practice, and the dynamic between classroom learning and simulation practice is key to the learning process in the course. Before the student completes a simulation, such as a chambers conference with a trial court judge in a civil matter, the teaching objectives are fully explained in this text and the simulated case file materials, and key concepts are presented in the video demonstration. As the simulated case files proceed through the semester or academic year, students receive time-released information on a condensed schedule designed to mimic the patterns of case development in legal practice. The classroom and the simulation group provide complimentary means of understanding the conceptual knowledge and professional skills needed to master the iterative process of discovering new facts, refining legal research objectives and managing the relationship with the client.

The authors are committed to continually improving the student experience in the course. Student engagement also means student critique and creative feedback. If you have a concern with or idea for improvement of the course materials, we encourage you to contact us at: coxxx211@umn.edu (Professor Cox) or thom0800@umn.edu (Professor Thomas).

P.C. & L.T.

January 2014

TABLE OF CONTENTS

LAW IN PRACTICE

CHAPTER 1

INTRODUCTION

■ ■ ■

The work of an attorney demands a variety of skills that are neither intuitive nor commonly possessed by young attorneys. The starting point in developing those skills is learning the basic legal doctrines that permeate the language of the law, such as contract and tort, and gaining the ability to conduct legal research and engage in legal reasoning.

Knowing relevant legal authority and reasoning is an essential part of practicing law, but only a part. Few attorneys go through an entire month without consulting statutes, case law or other sources of law. Yet few practicing attorneys spend most of their time conducting legal research. The law is intertwined with and forms the background against which attorneys advise clients, interview witnesses, and develop strategies for resolving disputes or closing transactions.

This text is about transforming your emerging knowledge of legal doctrine and reasoning into an introductory understanding of the practice of law—about how to use law in practice. Practicing attorneys must develop skills that transform legal knowledge into professional expertise that provides value to clients and allows the attorney to command an income for providing legal services. This chapter introduces some of the concepts and techniques underlying the skills taught in the simulation exercises, readings and videos that comprise this course.

1.1 THE IMPORTANCE OF LEGAL KNOWLEDGE

Clients seek out attorneys who know the law. Clients usually search for an attorney with specialized legal knowledge. A company wanting to issue new stock will seek an attorney who knows securities law. A consumer overwhelmed by debt may look for a bankruptcy attorney. Many problems, however, require legal expertise that you have already acquired. Consider the situation below.

> Nowecki Dry Cleaners receives about $1,100,000 in revenue each year and earns about $150,000 in net profit. Nowecki signed a written contract with CleanChem Company (3C) to buy a necessary and often used dry cleaning solution at $50 per pound for a period of 3 years starting on January 1, 2010. This price was over the market rate of $45 per pound in January 2010, but

1

Nowecki's owner was concerned about having predictable costs for the next few years. Other than employee costs, this chemical solution is the largest recurring expense of the business. Nowecki uses about 1,500 pounds per year of the solution and thus planned on spending about $75,000 for this solution each year from 2010 through 2012 under the contract with 3C.

In December 2011, the market price of the solution rose to $110 after political problems in West Africa prevented the export of one of the key components of the solution. 3C told Nowecki that effective January 1, 2012 it would no longer sell Nowecki the chemical at $50 per pound, but rather "will be forced by unforeseeable market conditions" to charge Nowecki $110 per pound. Nowecki objected, but 3C would not budge.

     a. Assume that you did not go to law school, but rather you own Nowecki Dry Cleaners. Would you retain an attorney to help you resolve this dispute? Why or why not?

     b. Assume that you are a licensed attorney, and Nowecki Dry Cleaners retains you in January, 2012. What claim does Nowecki have against 3C? What remedy would you seek for Nowecki if you asserted that claim in a Complaint?

Knowledge of the law allows an attorney to advise Nowecki about options for how to proceed, provides leverage to negotiate a settlement with 3C, and gives an attorney the basis to commence a lawsuit or arbitration if necessary. Attorneys offer unique value to their clients by translating the client's problem and experience into a matter of rights or obligations under the law.

1.2 THE ITERATIVE PROCESS OF FACT DEVELOPMENT AND LEGAL RESEARCH

In the *Phantom Toll Booth*, a book by architect Norton Juster, the protagonist is a child named Milo caught between the worlds of Digitopolis and Dictionopolis.[1] The citizens of Digitopolis understand the world only in numbers; the citizens of Dictionopolis value only words. Milo visits one world then the other world and finds their limited range of expression puzzling. Ultimately, Milo teaches the two worlds the value of understanding through both means of expression.

Legal education can be similarly one-dimensional at its beginning. Facts appear fully developed and discourse mostly is limited to understanding and manipulating legal doctrine as it appears in appellate cases.

---

[1] NORTON JUSTER, THE PHANTOM TOLLBOOTH (1961). Mr. Juster was a Professor of Architecture and Design at Hampshire College, as well as a practicing architect for much of his career.

Professors alter those given facts by posing hypothetical situations that force the student to test the boundaries of the doctrine. This is how law students learn the elements of contract formation, for example. The Nowecki Dry Cleaners situation is the type of problem routinely presented in a law school class or exam. The facts are recited and the student's task is to recall the proper legal doctrine and apply it to the facts of the case.

The actual practice of law more often occurs in reverse—the attorney starts with a base of legal knowledge and then gathers facts from the client and other sources. The attorney typically knows only the general nature of the client's concerns at the outset. For example, the client wants an estate plan or has been sued for employment discrimination. Attorneys have to gather facts that will be used to advise and represent the client. Fact gathering mostly consists of finding people with relevant knowledge and asking questions, or discovering and evaluating documents.

Once the attorney obtains enough facts to form a sufficient understanding of the problem or dispute, she uses her knowledge of the law to advise the client. As the facts of the matter develop in the course of the dispute or transaction, the attorney often will need to engage in legal research to identify possible claims or concerns and to evaluate how the law applies to her current understanding of the facts. This legal research, in turn, can raise questions that are resolvable only by gathering additional facts. In a case of any complexity, the attorney goes back and forth repeatedly between the requirements of the law and searching for facts.

As with Milo in the *Phantom Toll Booth*, attorneys are required to live in and mediate between two worlds. Attorneys must understand the world of abstract legal knowledge while also engaging with people and documents particular to each matter. Success in the practice of law lies substantially in mastering this iterative process of fact development and legal analysis.

1.2.1 A MODEL OF INITIAL CLAIM EVALUATION

The starting point for employing the fact-law iterative dynamic is an initial case evaluation. Experienced attorneys confronting a new case within their area of expertise often take the facts gathered at the outset of the case, perform a quick initial judgment about possible claims and then determine if further factual investigation or legal research is warranted or possible before consulting with the client about how to proceed. Beginning attorneys, on the other hand, are more like students of a foreign language. The translation of a client's narrative into the language of law requires a more conscious effort.

This section introduces a simplified four-step model for the process of performing an initial evaluation of possible legal claims in a dispute setting. The model is presented from the point of view of the potential plaintiff in a dispute. It can apply with minor adjustment to the evaluative process for defendants in disputes or to the work of attorneys in transactional matters.[2]

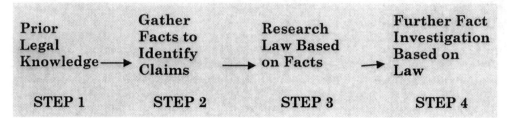

Red	Law
Blue	Fact Development

Figure 1–1.

Step #1: <u>Knowledge of the Law</u>. The attorney starts with knowledge of the area of law relevant to the client's problem. A principal job of law students is acquiring the legal knowledge needed to represent clients competently. In this course, you will learn the law necessary to help your client in the simulated cases.

Step #2: <u>Acquire the Facts Necessary to Identify Possible Legal Claims</u>. Your knowledge of the law shapes the information that you should obtain from the client or others to evaluate whether the client has a valid legal claim, or the relevant strength of multiple possible claims. Most cases begin with an interview of the client and perhaps other individuals critical to the case, such as the client's employees, co-workers, or witnesses to an event. You also will want to review any documents, research public records and collect any other readily available facts bearing on the case. Your job is not just to find out generally what happened. You want to know specific facts that will help you determine whether you can prove the elements of possible legal claims <u>or</u> defenses. Your inquiry should be shaped by the proof that is relevant to the claims you will evaluate.

Step #3: <u>Evaluation of Claims and Remedies—Back to the Law</u>. Sometimes the initial fact gathering will yield a simple, clear answer. In many cases, the information revealed will

---

[2] In some situations, of course, the dispute does not break down neatly into one possible plaintiff and one possible defendant—either party or multiple parties could bring a lawsuit or initiate arbitration.

require you to carefully consider how the facts fit the law you already know or areas of law about which you are less familiar. It is common to seek case law for guidance on how the elements of a claim or defense have been interpreted, or to conduct legal research on new claims or defenses that you had not previously considered. You also may consult other attorneys about the facts presented and evaluate possible legal claims for which you do not have substantial expertise.[3] As part of this step, you should be able to create a chart that shows the elements of each claim and the facts relevant to each element.[4]

Step #4: <u>Create a Strategy for Further Fact Investigation</u>. You may have enough information at this point to determine whether there exists a good faith allegation of a claim or claims, whether the facts strongly or weakly support each possible claim, and what facts will be most important in resolving the dispute. This knowledge will give you direction to engage in further fact gathering to strengthen your case, but with greater focus. Creating a chart of the relevant facts known for each element of each claim can aid in identifying where your claim lacks factual support.

Now you can develop a plan to search for facts, or evaluate the costs of acquiring facts, that are of the greatest consequence to the claims central to resolution of the matter. But you will return to fact gathering with a sharper focus. You will be seeking more specific information when conducting additional interviews of the client and others, in planning future discovery or in searching out other sources of facts, such as location visits or consulting experts.

Notice how this four-step process differs from the analysis that occurs in the usual law school class and exam. Instead of beginning with a complete set of facts, the starting point is knowledge of the law. This legal knowledge allows the attorney to engage the client and others in seeking specific information needed to evaluate possible legal claims and remedies. Rather than ending with a judgment on the validity of claims under the appropriate legal doctrine, the evaluative process sets the stage for further fact investigation.

---

[3] Or the attorney may seek to partner with other attorneys who have expertise in the matters presented by the client, or refer the case to other attorneys.

[4] The attorney will also evaluate possible remedies at this stage of the process. *See* chapter 8.

1.2.2 CONTINUING ITERATIVE DEVELOPMENT OF FACTS AND LAW

This iterative process of developing facts and engaging in legal research usually continues throughout a case because cases shift. A real estate transaction may be proceeding smoothly until the parties discover a gas station was located on the site fifty years ago and everyone now has to consider the possibility that the soil contains hidden pollutants. Discovery in litigation can unearth documents that convert a claim you thought of marginal value into the focus of a much bigger case with possible punitive damages. Just the opposite can occur. A claim you considered strong can be completely undone by the discovery of documents that undermine critical facts. Or a simple scheduling conference can result in an off-hand comment by the judge about the merits of the case that gives substantial negotiating leverage to one side or the other.

The emergence of new facts in a case, or the realization that facts on which the attorney relied are not accurate or persuasive, will force the attorney to re-evaluate the strength of claims in litigation or the risks in a transaction. For example, an attorney who represents an employer sued for racial discrimination may be relying on a former colleague of the plaintiff who claimed in an informal interview to have heard the plaintiff say that she was going to sue the company mostly because the company could afford to give her a good settlement and she needed the money. When called to testify at a deposition, the former colleague provides testimony that is ambiguous as to whether the plaintiff made such a statement. Now the attorney will have to decide whether to seek authority from the client to settle the lawsuit on less favorable terms, to continue searching for other facts to bolster the defense, or to just proceed with the current strategy because the former colleague's testimony is not essential to the company's defense of the discrimination claim. Similarly, as the court makes rulings or as the goals of the litigants or parties to a transaction change, the prior legal analysis and fact development strategy employed by the attorney may need re-evaluation.

Chapters 2–5 of this text focus on the skills needed to effectively develop facts. Chapter 2 discusses basic interviewing techniques. Chapters 3 and 4 elaborate on interviewing clients and witnesses, respectively. Chapter 5 explores the somewhat different set of questioning skills needed to build a written record when deposing a witness. These chapters, along with the skill-building video series, provide a base of knowledge designed to help you effectively engage in the simulations that form Unit I of the course—a client interview, a witness interview and a deposition.

1.3 CLIENTS

The evolving nature of most cases means that attorneys are constantly making strategic decisions. Do my client's concerns about the potential employee leaving after the completion of training justify inserting a covenant not to compete in the contract? Is a motion to compel discovery worth filing? Attorneys do not make such strategic decisions in isolation. A strategic decision should be based on a desired outcome, and the desired outcome requires understanding the goals of the client.

The attorney-client relationship is at the core of all the work performed by an attorney. Of course, clients usually pay your bill. Clients typically have information you want to obtain through a skillful interview (and that the other side may be able to obtain in a deposition or through other discovery mechanisms). Negotiation happens after the attorney works with the client to develop desired and acceptable options for resolving a dispute or completing a transaction. Chapter 3 explores the skills needed to build a trusting relationship with the client, starting with the first impressions created in the initial interview. Chapter 11 includes a discussion of counseling clients to prepare a negotiating strategy for mediation. Chapter 14 returns to client counseling in a transactional negotiation.

Your relationship with the client exists within the context of governing law. As an agent for the client, you owe the client fiduciary duties, such as the duty of loyalty. As a professional, you are subject to being sued for malpractice by your client. As a licensed attorney, the rules of professional responsibility circumscribe your relationship with the client. Chapter 6 explores the law and practice governing the attorney-client relationship, especially the attorney's ethical obligations to the client under professional responsibility rules. Chapter 14 looks at the process of forming the attorney-client relationship.

1.4 DISPUTE RESOLUTION AND ADVOCACY

Unless the attorney represents a client in a legal planning or advice matter involving no other parties, the client is not the only decision-maker of consequence to the attorney. The attorney may meet with a judge and perhaps a jury, with counsel for the opposing party or parties, and often with other people, such as a mediator. Interactions with each of these people offer an opportunity to engage in advocacy on behalf of the client in an effort to resolve the dispute or complete a transaction on favorable terms.

Chapters 7 and 8 introduce the core skills of advocacy and negotiation needed to effectively represent clients in dispute resolution. The next three chapters focus on the following particular tasks that employ advocacy and negotiating skills: drafting or responding to a written settlement offer letter in Chapter 9; appearing before a judge in chambers in Chapter 10; and participating in a mediation conducted by a qualified neutral in Chapter 11. These chapters correspond to the simulations that comprise Unit II of the course.

1.5 THE CONTEXT OF LEGAL PRACTICE

Attorneys practice law in a vast array of subject areas and contexts. What does an attorney working on large corporate merger transactions in a 2,000 lawyer firm in Chicago, Illinois have in common with a personal injury attorney in solo practice in Corvallis, Oregon? A lot, actually. The need to develop facts within the framework of law, the importance of the client relationship, and the need to engage in advocacy cut across almost all legal work. Yet the context in which the attorney practices obviously shapes the exercise of those skills.

This text uses a common dividing point for types of legal practice— litigation or transactional work. Litigators represent clients in disputes; transactional attorneys help clients complete deals or plan their business activities to comply with the law. Obviously, there are attorneys whose practice is not captured accurately by this short-hand distinction, but cleaving the practice of law into these two parts conveys a divide that helps explain critical differences in how attorneys employ the skills of legal practice.

The simulations associated with Units I and II of the course are based on a litigation case file, while the simulations associated with the Unit III of the course are based on a transaction case file. The final three chapters of the text discuss the application of basic interviewing, counseling, and negotiation skills to the circumstances faced by the transactional attorney. Chapter 12 introduces transactional law and how transactional attorneys differ from litigators in thought process and culture. Chapter 13 introduces a more complex and nuanced concept of "integrative negotiation," which opens up the possibility of creating value rather than just distributing value in negotiations. Chapter 14 examines client counseling when engaging in integrative negotiations, with an emphasis on the work of the transactional attorney.

Unfortunately or not, the most important factor in determining how attorneys exercise their skill in a case usually is related to money. To put it bluntly but without overstatement, the amount of money available to pay legal fees controls the extent to which the attorney can engage in fact gathering and legal analysis. As a former criminal prosecutor and later civil litigator stated, "justice can be different depending on what your wallet says."[5] A criminal defense attorney's ability to develop facts will

---

[5] Gretchen Morgenson, *He Felled a Giant, but He Can't Collect*, N.Y. TIMES, July 1, 2012, at BU1 (quoting Charles T. Matthews).

look wholly different if she is a public defender representing dozens of indigent defendants simultaneously versus representing a few affluent white collar defendants. An average person with a $1,500 claim for faulty car repairs probably will need to learn how to use small claims court. Unless a statute provides for attorney's fee recovery for such a plaintiff, an attorney's charge for recovering on the claim likely will exceed the amount of the recovery. As you complete the simulations associated with this course, consider how the case would proceed differently if the dollar amounts involved were a fraction of the amount actually at issue, or a multiple of many times more than the actual amount.[6]

---

[6] The adaptation of advanced information technology to legal services offers the potential to change the high cost of legal services, as well as presents important issues about the structure of the legal profession in coming decades. For an excellent overview of the changes being wrought in the legal profession by technology and outside pressures, *see* RICHARD SUSSKIND, TOMORROW'S LAWYER'S: AN INTRODUCTION TO YOUR FUTURE (2013). The legal profession also is changing itself to address the disparity between the surplus of practicing attorneys and the lack of access to legal services for the less affluent. *See, e.g., In the Matter of the Adoption of New APR 28*, Order 25700–A-1005, Washington Supreme Court (June 15, 2012) (creating a Board to issue "Limited Legal License Technicians" to provide legal services in legal specialties for which the general public is underserved).

CHAPTER 2

FUNDAMENTAL QUESTIONING TECHNIQUES

▪ ▪ ▪

"I was a wonderful parent before I had children," states an author of parenting books.[1] So it is with interviewing. You know how to talk to other people, as you have been doing for as long as you remember. Effectively interviewing people in a professional setting, however, demands skills not acquired through casual conversation.

Interviewing is a core skill of most professions. Architects, realtors, doctors, police officers and other professionals who interact with people rely on interviews to perform their jobs. Attorneys are no different. Whether litigating a case or putting together a deal, attorneys routinely engage in interviews of clients, witnesses, experts and others. Studies suggest that attorneys spend more time interviewing people than almost any other task—more than twice as much time as conducting legal research.[2] Unfortunately, the same studies also suggest that attorneys generally do not conduct effective interviews.[3]

Interviews conducted by attorneys serve the dual purpose of developing a constructive relationship with the interviewee and acquiring information that the attorney needs to conduct the representation. This chapter

---

[1] ADELE FABER & ELAINE MAZLISH, HOW TO TALK SO KIDS WILL LISTEN & LISTEN SO KIDS WILL TALK 1 (1980).

[2] Don Peters & Martha M. Peters, *Maybe That's Why I Do That: Psychological Type Theory, The Myers-Briggs Type Indicator, and Learning Legal Interviewing*, 35 N.Y.L. SCH. REV. 169, 170 n.4 (1990) (stating that attorneys devote more time to interviewing clients that any other professional activity); Avrom Hirsh Sherr, Competence and Skill Acquisition in Lawyer Client Interviewing 44 (Aug. 1991) (unpublished Ph.D. thesis, University of Warwick) (available at wrap.warwick.ac.uk/2541/1/WRAP_THESIS_Sherr_1991.pdf) (finding that British solicitors spend about 13% of their time interviewing clients, but no more than 5.5% of their time conducting legal research).

[3] New attorneys tend to fail miserably at basic interviewing techniques, especially at creating rapport with the client and at eliciting the client's story through open-end questions Sherr, *supra* note 2, at 58–104; Peters & Peters, *supra* note 2, at 169. Other studies have shown that attorneys tend to be too controlling and uninterested in the message the client is conveying. Austin Sarat & William L.F. Felstiner, *Lawyers and Legal Consciousness: Law Talk in the Divorce Lawyer's Office*, 98 YALE L. J. 1663 (1989) (study of attorney-client conversations in the course of divorce cases); Carl J Hosticka, *We Don't Care What Happened, We Only Care About What is Going to Happen: Lawyer-Client Negotiations of Reality*, 26 SOC. PROBS. 598 (1979) (study of initial interviews between legal aid attorneys and indigent clients); Gary Neustadter, *When Lawyer and Client Meet: Observations of interviewing and Counseling Behavior in the Consumer Bankruptcy Law Office*, 35 BUFF. L. REV. 177 (1986) (study of consumer bankruptcy attorney's initial consultation with clients).

focuses on questioning techniques that attorneys use to maximize information from the client, witness or other interviewee for the purpose of evaluating legal issues in the case.   Chapter 3 examines client interviews, including how to discern client goals.   Chapter 4 looks at the unique issues involved with witness interviews.

2.1 OBTAINING RELEVANT AND IMPORTANT FACTS

A key difference in fact gathering interviews between attorneys and other professions is that attorneys seek facts to evaluate or prove legal claims and defenses. Attorneys gather facts to make judgments about the law. An attorney with a client seeking estate planning help will inquire about the client's assets, current and projected income, and other financial information that will determine the legal options for structuring the client's estate instruments.   The law firm associate returning from a witness interview related to a case in litigation should be prepared to tell the partner or litigation team about what she learned from the witness that bears on the critical elements of the law at issue in the dispute.

Consider how the job of the attorney differs from the interviewing task facing two other professions—medicine and journalism—in the context of a toxic leak incident.   A container holding methane chemicals at a fertilizer plant near Ocala, Florida was damaged in a severe storm. The plant is owned and operated by Bi-Tell Industries. The workers at the plant failed to notice that after the storm a microscopic crack had opened in the outside shell of the container.   Over the next few weeks, a tiny quantity of moisture leaked through the tank and the safety systems failed to prevent water from reaching the chemicals. As a result, a small amount of toxic gas escaped into the surrounding community. About a dozen people living in the area near the plant experienced eye irritation and respiratory difficulties, and some of these people became seriously ill.

Bridget McDonald is a 25 year woman who lived near the plant and was sickened by the toxic gas.   At the plant, Nathan Kalanick was the Supervisor who had primary responsibility for maintaining the safety of the container. Mr. Kalanick was at the plant at the time of the release, but he did not become sick because his office was upwind from the tank. You have the opportunity to interview both Ms. McDonald and Mr. Kalanick. Consider the following scenarios:

> (1) You are a doctor or medical assistant interviewing each of these people on the day Ms. McDonald appears at the emergency room of your hospital. What do you want to know from Ms. McDonald and Mr. Kalanick to help you treat Ms. McDonald?

> (2) You are a journalist interviewing each of these people on the day when Ms. McDonald and her neighbors become ill. What do

you want to know from Ms. McDonald and Mr. Kalanick to file a story that afternoon?

(3) You are an attorney. Ms. McDonald hires you to represent her to obtain compensation for her injuries. Based on the above facts and your legal education to date, what are the likely claims that Ms. McDonald may have against Bi-Tell? What questions do you want to ask Ms. McDonald that will help you determine the viability and value of her possible claims against Bi-Tell? If you have the opportunity to conduct discovery on Bi-Tell, including taking the deposition of Mr. Kalanick, what will you want to discover?

The objectives of each professional shape the information that person will attempt to obtain from those involved in the incident. The doctor or medical assistant will want to collect information that assists in the prompt treatment of Ms. McDonald, such as what type of gas was released, the length of time and quantity of possible exposure by Ms. McDonald, the symptoms experienced by Ms. McDonald, and her medical history. The journalist will want information that informs the community about the extent, causes and consequence of the release, such as the type of gas released and its possible effects, any immediate or long-term safety concerns for residents of the area, and the reason for the accident, among other things.

The attorney is interested in some of the same content as the doctor or journalist, but also different information that corresponds to the requirements of possible legal claims that can be asserted on behalf of Ms. McDonald. Think about how your inquiry as an attorney would overlap with and differ from the questions posed by the doctor or journalist. The remainder of this text will return to the experience of the attorney working with Ms. McDonald to provide examples of the attorney's need for information in this situation. At every point in the process of fact gathering, the attorney is forced to consider how the facts he has discovered or wants to discover will shape the meaning of the law as applied in that case.

2.2 QUESTION FORMATION: OPEN-END AND PROBING QUESTIONS

Once the attorney understands the information needed to evaluate legal claims or issues, she will need to think about interviewing techniques that help her obtain that information. The form of questions can determine what information the interviewee provides to the attorney.

2.2.1   OPEN-END AND CLOSED-END QUESTIONS

Was the first chapter of this text too long or too short? This question begs for a short, definitive answer—the first chapter was too long, too short, or just about the right length. Perhaps you have a useful opinion about how the first chapter could be improved, but asking you about the length of the chapter is not an effective means of discovering your ideas for improving the first chapter.

The above question is "closed." The alternative is an open-end question. Consider these examples:

Open-end	Closed-end
What happened at the restaurant?	Did you see Olson at the restaurant?
How did you feel when Olson left?	Were you upset that Olson left?
Tell me about the accident?	Were you the driver when the accident occurred?
What else do you remember?	Is that all you remember?

Open-end questions encourage the interviewee to share knowledge, beliefs and attitudes. Closed-end questions beg for a yes or no answer, or a one-word or one-phrase response.

You will want to use both open-end and closed-end questions, depending on the circumstances. Unless you have a specific reason for wanting only responses to narrowly tailored questions throughout the interview, it is usually best to start with broad and open-end questions. Open-end questions provide the greatest opportunity to obtain the interviewee's knowledge of events and perspective on the matter.

2.2.2   PROBING QUESTIONS

Probing questions seek to obtain information the interviewee does not (or will not) freely recall and volunteer. A useful construct for thinking about probing questions is to search the list of familiar interrogatories—who, what, when, where, why and how. You can use these interrogatories to create probing questions that elicit all of the information that the interviewee possesses about the subject and is willing to share.

For instance, if an attorney wants to learn all of the movies that you have watched in the last three months, he might start with a general inquiry, such as the obvious question, "What movies have you seen in the last three months?" Take a break from reading and make a list.

Now let's probe your recent movie watching a bit. Answer the specific questions below, assuming that each answer is limited to your activity in the last three months. As you answer the questions, add to your list of movies watched if the questions trigger any memory of a movie not already on the list.

> What types of movies have you watched? Comedies? Dramas? Horror? Non-English movies (if so, what languages and from what countries)?

> Where have you seen movies? Have you gone to a theater to see movies (if yes, details)? Have you seen movies somewhere other than your home or a theater (if yes, details as to where and when and with whom)?

> Tell me about how you acquire movies that you have watched outside of a theater? Have you acquired movies from a site on the internet (if so, what sites)? If you pay for such movies, how do you pay for movies that you download/stream? Have you watched movies from your downloaded collection? Have you borrowed movies from the collection of friends or family?

> When have you watched movies? Have you seen any movies other than during the evening hours? Have you watched movies during a vacation from school or work? Have you watched movies during a holiday gathering?

> Why do you watch movies? Have you watched any movies for a reason other than personal enjoyment? Movies related to school or work, for example? Have you watched any movies because of reading a positive review? Have you watched any movies because of hearing that the movie won an award or was nominated for an award?

> With whom have you watched movies? Have you watched movies with friends present? With family present? Who are your favorite actors? Have you seen any movies starring any of these actors?

Notice how these probing questions do more than add to your movie list (if that occurred). These questions also provide a growing base of information which can be used to find out what movies you watch or verify your answers. For example, if you answered that you pay for movies with a credit card or that you use particular downloading or delivery services for obtaining movies, you also likely have presented to the interviewer the possibility of using your credit card records, download or other computer records, or similar sources to verify or further investigate your responses.[4]

Use the familiar interrogatory questions to help you think about everything you want to know about specific events or statements by an

---

[4] Also notice that probing questions can be either open-end or closed-end. Section 2.4.1 discusses how to use both types of questions in probing for detailed information.

interviewee. If a witness tells you that he had a conversation with the opposing party, how would you probe for the details of that conversation? Again, stop and make a list of questions.

Some of the questions that could be on that list are as follows: When did the conversation occur? How was the conversation conducted (by phone, in person)? Why were you talking with that person at that time? If it was an in-person conversation, where did it take place? What specifically was said by each party? Why did you (or the other person) say "x"? Was anyone else present (if so, whom)?

Compare this type of probing inquiry to everyday discussions. If your neighbor mentions that he talked to a mutual friend, you probably will not unleash the above barrage of probing questions. That would be odd in casual conversation. An important distinction between interviewing in a professional capacity and casual conversation is the need to obtain detailed information from the interviewee through the use of probing questions.

It is difficult to overstate the value of learning how to ask extensive probing questions to obtain from an interviewee all of the information she possesses about topics of importance to the attorney. Yet the extent of a probing inquiry by the attorney will be limited by the context of the interview. The amount of detailed questioning depends on the relationship of the attorney and the interviewee, the amount of time either person has to devote to the interview and other factors.

As discussed in Section 2.1, the attorney is interested in information relevant to the legal concerns presented by the case. He usually will not have time to probe every detail known by the client or witness that may conceivably be relevant. There may be no harm in asking Ms. McDonald what she was wearing on the day of the gas exposure, but this information likely will be of no consequence in evaluating her personal injury claim. When representing a criminal defendant who claims to have been wrongly identified as the perpetrator, questions about clothing worn on the day of the crime would be quite relevant. The attorney focuses probing questions on the most relevant matters to the legal claims and defenses at issue.

2.3 STAGES OF AN INTERVIEW

Interviews can be organized in different ways depending on the person being interviewed, the subject matter and constraints of time or place. Many commentators have noted that interviews can be seen as occurring in four stages: introductory, narrative, probing and concluding.[5]

---

[5] *See, e.g.,* STEFAN H. KRIEGER & RICHARD K. NEUMANN, JR., ESSENTIAL LAWYERING SKILLS: INTERVIEWING, COUNSELING, NEGOTIATION, AND PERSUASIVE FACT ANALYSIS 97–99 (4th ed. 2011).

2.3.1   INTRODUCTORY

An interview is a human interaction and the interviewee likely will respond positively to a warm and personal beginning, such as "small-talk" about the trip to the office. As obvious as this point may seem, a certain number of professionals omit this important step in the interview. Until the medical profession broadly recognized the importance of quality human interaction in effective treatment, it was not uncommon for a busy doctor to meet a new patient in an examining room and say something like, "I am Dr. Alexis— let me see the rash you are complaining about." Medical schools now typically have extensive training programs to teach the skill of interviewing patients.[6]

Attorneys almost always have specific information that they must or should convey at the beginning of an interview. When meeting a new client or potential client, the attorney will want to discuss the creation of the attorney-client relationship and important precepts of that relationship, such as confidentiality. A detailed explanation of this aspect of the initial client interview is contained in Chapter 14. The first client interview simulation in this course assumes that the attorney-client relationship has already been formed. Section 4.3.1 discusses the ethical obligations of an attorney at the beginning of an interview with an unrepresented witness.

2.3.2   INTERVIEWEE NARRATIVE

There is a lot of value, and very little downside, to beginning an interview by letting the client or witness tell his or her story, with encouragement from open-end questions by the attorney. The interviewee will have a chance to use his own words and offer his unique perspective when prompted to provide his own narrative at the start of the discussion.

Studies have shown that learning to ask open-end questions can substantially increase the amount of information shared by an interviewee. British researchers, for instance, trained police officers in different interviewing techniques and then measured the impact of the training on the ability of the officers to obtain information as compared to a control group with no training. The officers who markedly increased use of open-ended questions (from 4% to 42% of questions) showed a

---

[6] WILLIAM M. SULLIVAN ET AL., EDUCATING LAWYERS: PREPARATION FOR THE PROFESSION OF LAW 81, 192 (2007). The medical profession also has begun to question patients about their interaction with the doctor to improve the delivery of medical services. Clark D. Cunningham, *Evaluating Effective Lawyer-Client Communication: An International Project Moving from Research to Reform*, 67 FORDHAM L. REV. 1959, 1959–60 (1999) (Once in practice, physicians learn from periodic surveys of their patients that evaluate satisfaction with the doctor.).

"large increase" in the amount of information obtained in suspect and witness interviews.[7]

Open-end questions to prompt narrative answers at the beginning of an interview also mitigate the problem of limiting the information provided by the interviewee due to attorney assumptions and biases. Young attorneys frequently make the incorrect assumption that what the client or witness is saying about an event is incontrovertibly true and thus do not search out information from that interviewee or others that would contradict this "fact." Unnecessary limits on the information acquired also occur because the attorney and the interviewee do not share the same life experiences, so implications that seem obvious for the attorney to draw may not be the intended communication of the client. Or the attorney may make premature judgments about the client's goals or the interviewee's situation, thus discouraging the interviewee from sharing useful facts or perspectives.

Consider the example of a client who arrives at a legal aid office and starts talking about her home going into foreclosure. The attorney might immediately begin to ask questions designed to determine if the client has a foreclosure defense. The client's mention of foreclosure, however, may just be prefatory to talking about the threatened garnishment of her bank account for credit card debts. Perhaps she is ready to abandon the house, but needs to preserve cash to obtain rental housing. Starting the interview with open-end questions and allowing the interviewee to fully explain her view of the events or problems that bring her to the interview helps prevent a premature diagnosis.

In a 2008 study, researchers observed and recorded five experienced attorneys interview a mock client. Interviews by two attorneys with markedly different styles were contrasted. Attorney A let the client tell her story with few interruptions at the start of the interview, while Attorney B's interview "was full of interruptions and dominated by the attorney." Attorney A obtained more useful information about the client's situation and the client's goals than Attorney B. Interestingly, this process of letting the client tell the attorney about the situation without substantial interruption was more efficient. Attorney A completed the interview in less time and gained all of the essential facts of the client's narrative.[8]

2.3.3 PROBING

The attorney probes for more detailed information from the client during the third stage of the interview. This part of the interview usually is the

---

[7] Brian R. Clifford & Richard George, *A Field Evaluation of Training in Three Methods of Witness/Victim Investigative Interviewing*, 2 PSYCHOL., CRIME & L. 231, 237–240 (1996).

[8] Linda F. Smith, *Was It Good For You Too? Conversation Analysis of Two Interviews*, 96 KY L.J. 579 (2008).

most challenging and time-consuming. Section 2.4 below examines the probing stage of the interview.

2.3.4   CONCLUDING

The conclusion of the interview is an opportunity for the attorney to further build an appropriate and effective relationship with the interviewee. The interviewer can review some of the key information learned during the interview to make sure the information is accurate, but also to communicate to the interviewee that the interviewer was paying close attention during the conversation. The concluding moments of the interview also can be used to reiterate any promises made by either person about completing tasks following the interview, such as providing contact information for a person mentioned or a copy of a document discussed during the interview.

As obvious as it may seem in the abstract, it is again important to remember the basic courtesies of human interaction when concluding the interview. All too often an attorney will just say, "that's all I have to ask for now," or the like. If it is appropriate, the attorney should thank the interviewee for taking the time to travel to meet the attorney.

2.4 CONDUCTING THE PROBING STAGE OF THE INTERVIEW

The probing stage of the interview requires the attorney to translate her need for information proving (or disproving) specific elements of a claim or defense into the best questions for acquiring that information. This section examines the use of an open-probe questioning technique for accomplishing this objective. This section also discusses the attorney's organization of topics to cover during this stage of the interview.

2.4.1   OPEN-PROBE QUESTIONING TECHNIQUE

Open-end and probing questions can be combined throughout the probing interview stage to fully explore the knowledge of the interviewee. We will call this the "open-probe" method of questioning. Combining open-end and probing questions during this stage of the interview is commonly considered by commentators an effective technique for the probing stage of attorney interviews.[9]

As noted above, it usually will be productive to start the interview by asking very broad open-end questions that permit the interviewee to tell you about his or her perspective on the event, problem or opportunity that

---

[9] One of the primary texts on attorney skill development comprehensively and effectively describes this concept of combining open and closed questions as the "T-funnel technique." DAVID A. BINDER, ET. AL., LAWYERS AS COUNSELORS: A CLIENT CENTERED APPROACH 169–184 (3d ed. 2012).

you are investigating. You may want to keep the interviewee sharing information by asking encouraging open-end questions, such as, "tell me what happened next?" or "what else occurred?."

When the interviewee has exhausted his or her initial sharing of information, you can move to exploring specific topics in more depth. For each topic (or sub-topic) you want to explore, start with an open-end question. Continue encouraging open-end questions about that topic as appropriate and productive. Then transition to probing questions that explore details about the topic. When you have exhausted probing the topic, it is often useful to finish with a question like, "is there anything else about (topic) that we have not discussed?"

For example, in the toxic release case described in Section 2.1, both sides will want to inquire about the extent of injury suffered by Ms. McDonald. If you represent Ms. McDonald, you will need to establish damages to prove your claim, and the amount of damages recoverable will depend largely on the degree of injury suffered by Ms. McDonald. Imagine that in the initial part of the interview Ms. McDonald tells you that she experienced watering and itching in her eyes and that her nose was running, and she later developed breathing problems. After she had trouble breathing she went to the emergency room and the doctors put her on an intravenous drip with some kind of drug to counteract the toxic gas. She was in the hospital for three days.

Given the importance of the topic of Ms. McDonald's injuries to her case, you will want to explore several sub-topics related to her injury. You will want to inquire about her health before she became ill, the impact on her current and long-term physical condition, the pain she suffered during the exposure and its aftermath, any psychological disturbance caused by the experience, her loss of work and life disruption, her treatment by medical professionals (before and after the gas exposure), and her discussion with others about her injuries.

Let's focus on one of these sub-topics, her medical treatment after the gas exposure, and apply the open-probe method. You begin with an open-end question about the sub-topic, such as—"Tell me about the doctors you have seen since your exposure to the gas?" Ms. McDonald responds that she saw some doctors in the hospital and that after she left the hospital she has seen her general practitioner, Dr. Sharon Noreen, and a neurologist, Dr. Anwar Abodo. She tells you they all have been "really nice."

Now you want to ask probing questions about that experience. Let's focus on just one part of this treatment—her medical treatment after leaving the hospital. Take a break and write a list of all the probing questions that you would ask Ms. McDonald.

Below are some of the probing questions that you might consider asking Ms. McDonald:

> When did you first receive medical attention from Dr. Noreen? How many times did you see Dr. Noreen? When was the last time you saw Dr. Noreen? [Repeat for Dr. Abodo].

> What did Dr. (Noreen/Adobo) tell you about your condition?

> Why did you go to these particular doctors? Did someone refer you to them? Who?

> Have any of your doctors prescribed medications? What medications? [For each medication] When did you start taking this medication? Are you still taking any of these medications?

> What else did these doctors do to help you with your injuries? Were these treatments effective—are you feeling better?

> Have you seen any medical professionals after you left the hospital other than Dr. Noreen or Dr. Abodo? Someone like a physical therapist or mental health therapist? [If yes, explore]

When you have exhausted probing questions on this sub-topic, you can complete the inquiry by asking Ms. McDonald if there is anything about her treatment for gas exposure after leaving the hospital that you have not discussed. After all information is gained from Ms. McDonald on this sub-topic, you can move on to an open-end question on another sub-topic.

2.4.2   ORGANIZING BY LEGAL ELEMENTS OR CHRONOLOGY

The organization of this probing stage of the interview will depend on what the attorney wants to know, to whom the attorney is talking and the conversation style that is most comfortable and effective for that attorney. Two common methods of organizing the probing stage of the interview are by legal elements or by chronology.[10]

In a legal elements outline, the attorney breaks down the elements of claims or defenses that he or the opposing party must prove and denotes each as a topic, if appropriate for that interviewee. Some of these elements may require multiple sub-topics, as was true in the example interview of Ms. McDonald above. The open-probe questioning method usually will be more easily adapted to an inquiry organized by a legal elements analysis. Such an interview involves a series of topics well-suited to the process of eliciting narrative responses and then probing for details.

Chronological organization breaks down the interview into a timeline of the events of concern to the attorney. A chronological interview usually

---

[10] BINDER ET AL., *supra* note 9, at 111–206; KRIEGER & NEUMANN, *supra* note 5, at 149–168.

will rely more heavily on open-end questions, such as "what happened next?" Yet the attorney will also want to probe the details of the narrative responses to these questions with the familiar interrogatories. The attorney can consider each episode in the chronology as the beginning of a new topic that leads with an open-end question and should be followed by probing questions to elicit details of the events.

In practice, the attorney will want to acquire information responsive to either approach. She will want to be able to construct a timeline of events from the perspective of the interviewee at the end of the interview. She also will want to be able to identify all the information the interviewee can provide about the legal elements of claims or defenses.

One way to achieve these dual objectives is to select one approach and exhaust the interview. Then, use the other approach to review the information with the interviewee. For instance, the McDonald interview could proceed by a legal element model. At the conclusion of those questions, the attorney could use the information gained during the interview to create a timeline and have the interviewee confirm that the attorney's constructed timeline is accurate.

2.5 BUILDING RAPPORT IN INTERVIEWING

Effective attorney interviewers build rapport with an interviewee in the process of acquiring specific information needed to make legal judgments about the client's situation. Achieving these dual objectives requires the exercise of different skills and modes of thinking. Effective listening and communicating empathy draws more on personal relationship skills and holistic thinking, while awareness of gathering facts that prove or disprove specific legal elements draws more on the analytic and logical processing style. Yet building rapport with a client and obtaining the facts necessary to make legal judgments about the client's situation are mutually reinforcing processes.

Research on interviewing supports the value of this approach. For example, Australian researchers showed test subjects "a 66 second videotape...of a burning motor vehicle in a field and a male bystander watching from the side. This man suddenly runs and dives into the burning vehicle. There is an excited verbal interchange from off-screen bystanders, a fire truck arrives and further agitated conversations from off-screen bystanders ensue." After watching the video, three types of interviewers questioned the subjects about what they had observed using three different types of voice tone, body posture and the like. The three styles were labeled rapport building, abrupt and neutral. The results showed that "when the interviewer built rapport, participants provided more correct bits of information without a corresponding increase in incorrect bits of information."[11]   In short, interviewees who feel comfortable and heard are more likely to share information with the attorney.

We discuss above the technique of beginning the interview with open-ended questions and letting the interviewee tell his narrative. This is an efficient means to acquire information that also helps to minimize the problem of the attorney limiting the inquiry due to incorrect assumptions and bias. The narrative phase of the interview also can serve to build rapport and trust when the interviewee feels that the attorney is truly listening to his concerns. Commentators on legal interviewing encourage attorneys to develop engaged listening skills, including displaying empathy and paying attention to nonverbal communication.[12]

The key set of behaviors for engaged listening concern the interviewer's focus on the interviewee. Techniques include directly facing the interviewee and maintaining eye contact, appropriately reacting to the interviewee's disclosures, and reflecting back to the interviewee the gist of her responses.[13]

Some people find it easier to build rapport in an interview, just as some law students are quicker to adapt to the thought processes that underlie legal analysis and reasoning. Professor Neil Hamilton has developed a series of self-assessments tests to help law students "identify areas and situations in which they may have weaker listening skills and target them for improvement."[14] The test includes questions such as the following: whether the student looks at his cell phone during conversations; whether the student uses head nods and facial expressions to show that he is listening to the speaker; or whether the student constantly takes notes during conversations. If you are unsure of your disposition as an engaged listener, consider taking Professor Hamilton's self-assessment.

---

[11] Roger Collins, Robyn Lincoln & Mark G. Frank, *The Effect of Rapport in Forensic Interviewing*, 9 PSYCHIATRY PSYCHOL. & L. 69, 73–75 (2002).

[12] *See, e.g.*, KRIEGER & NEUMANN, *supra* note 5, at 91–95; BINDER ET AL., *supra* note 9, at 40–62; Linda F. Smith, *Client-Lawyer Talk: Lessons from Other Disciplines*, 13 CLINICAL L. REV. 505, 534 (2006). Professors Krieger and Neumann conclude that, "[t]he ability to listen well is as important in the practice of law as the ability to talk well." KRIEGER & NEUMANN, *supra* note 5, at 92.

[13] This last technique is known as "active listening," which will be familiar to any student of therapy. For a thorough explanation of the role of active listening in legal interviewing, see BINDER ET AL., *supra* note 9, at 40–62.

[14] Neil Hamilton, *Effectiveness Requires Listening: How To Assess and Improve Listening Skills*, 13 FLA. COASTAL L. REV. 145, 163 (2012).

CHAPTER 3

CLIENTS AND THE INITIAL CLIENT INTERVIEW

■ ■ ■

Attorneys are the agent in a principal-agent relationship. That means an attorney takes direction from his principal, the client. Successfully managing the attorney-client relationship will help you more effectively represent your clients. It also may determine whether you face sanction by the state licensing association,[1] enjoy your work, and have enough clients to prosper if you are in private practice.

In Chapter 2, you considered interviewing mostly from the perspective of the attorney. The attorney needs to know what she wants from an interview to help form judgments about how the law applies to the client's situation. Gathering these facts requires some thought about how to ask questions and how to organize the interview. Now we look at the interview from the perspective of the client and the attorney-client relationship. This chapter also briefly introduces the importance of considering diversity in representing clients.

3.1 CLIENT GOALS

Effective and ethical attorneys find out what their clients want and develop strategies that meet those goals. Part of the job of the initial interview is to discern the client's goals and have some sense of the client's priorities among those goals.

3.1.1 DETERMINING GOALS OF THE CLIENT

The client's desired outcomes can easily be described in some cases, especially when the case is primarily about a money loss. The client who has been sued for negligence in constructing a building likely will hope to avoid paying anything to the plaintiff, or to minimize any payment. In the Nowecki Dry Cleaners situation discussed in Section 1.1, the dry cleaner likely will want to recover money for CleanChem Company's breach of the supply contract.

---

[1] The relationship between the client and the attorney is circumscribed by the attorney's ethical obligations. An explanation of these obligations is set forth in Chapter 6.

Many clients also have non-monetary goals that need to be discovered by the attorney. Some of the more common non-monetary goals include the following:

* *Reputation.* The client may be concerned about how the matter will affect the client's reputation in the business community or with the general public. Examples: An employee is concerned that suing his former employer for wrongful termination will mark him as a "trouble-maker" and make it impossible to get another job in that profession. A financial institution is concerned that aggressively defending a class action alleging that it over-charged interest amounts to active duty soldiers will lead to adverse media stories that will hurt its reputation with consumers and public officials. A manufacturer aggressively defends a patent infringement suit to discourage others who might consider filing this type of suit against it in the future.

* *Relationships.* The client may want to protect personal or business relationships. Examples: A divorcing spouse wants to enhance the opportunity for a cooperative parenting relationship or preserve a relationship with former in-laws. A company attempting to purchase another company wants to construct the deal so as to maximize the good will of the acquired company's management. A supplier is concerned that pursuing litigation against another company will result in the loss of that company as a customer.

* *Ownership or Control.* The client may want to assert ownership or control over real estate, things, a company or a person. Examples: A putative seller tries to rescind a purchase agreement on his house, and the putative buyer wants to own this particular home with its unique characteristics rather than get monetary compensation. A person in a dispute over ownership of a family business highly values being declared the owner of more than half the stock so as to control the operations of the company.

* *Limit Disruption or Protect Privacy.* Some clients, particularly potential litigants, may be concerned about life or business disruption, or prefer not to be publicly exposed. Examples: A parent expresses concern about whether a child might have to testify in a child custody dispute. A closely held business states that it will view negatively any deal to sell the business that requires the owners to produce personal financial records.

* *Business Practice Regulation.* The client may want to require (or stop) certain marketing or operation practices by a business. Examples: A state environmental protection agency seeks to have a metal recycling plant cease discharging waste products into a nearby river. A non-profit serving the elderly wants another non-profit to cease using a similar trade name.

* *Vindication.* The client may want a judge or jury to decide the outcome or the client may want the opportunity to tell his story in court. <u>Examples</u>: A person suing for defamation wants a declaration by a jury that she was defamed. A whistleblower suing her former employer desires the satisfaction of publicly telling about the company's fraud.

3.1.2   PROBING THE CLIENT FOR A FULL UNDERSTANDING OF GOALS

Like questioning for fact gathering, the attorney will want to begin the discussion of client goals with open-ended questions, encouraging the client to provide a narrative of what the client would like to see happen. For example, the attorney may ask, "What is the best outcome for you in this dispute?" As with fact gathering, open-ended questions and eliciting a client narrative helps to protect against the attorney making unwarranted assumptions about the client's goals for the representation.

Unlike questioning for fact gathering, the "probing" stage of this inquiry usually should not involve questions shaped by familiar interrogatories which seek details of events that have already occurred or knowledge of particular matters. Rather, the attorney will want to help the client fully articulate any objectives or expectations about the matter of representation. The client's goals for the representation often can be more complex than one might assume on first hearing the problem.

Some clients know they have a problem, but have no clear idea how the problem can be resolved. Other clients will state multiple goals. These goals may be in substantial conflict. For instance, the client may state a desire to obtain the return of all money lost in a business transaction involving fraud, but also express an unwillingness to incur any disruption from litigation. Or multiple client goals can be wholly or partially consistent, as when the client wants compensation for property damage and a declaration that a neighbor's building has encroached on the client's property.

Whether the multiple goals are consistent or not, the attorney's primary responsibility is to discern the client's priorities among the goals. A rank ordering of goals can be useful in some cases, but perhaps more often the attorney will want a general sense at the outset of the case as to which goals are essential, which goals are strongly preferred and which goals are less important.

Determining and probing the client's goals in the initial interview is not the end of communicating with the client about desired outcomes. Client's goals can shift during the course of the representation. The client's goals can change because the process of litigating a case or constructing a deal reveals new information making the client more aware of risks, costs or burden in pursuing the matter. Or the goals can shift because of a change in external circumstance. A company seeking financing for solar energy panels on its buildings as a means to project an environmentally friendly reputation may acquire new management who focuses solely on the economic payback of the transaction.

The client's goals may not always dictate the most thorough and noteworthy legal work. Nor will the attorney's short-term interest and the client's interest always coincide. Winning at trial, for example, may represent a reputational victory for the attorney and large fees billable to the client. But if the cost of that victory is legal fees that swallow up most of the award and lost time for the client in trial and litigation preparation, the attorney's victory is unlikely to have met the goals of the client. The attorney's job is to represent the client, which includes performing legal work that meets the client's goals regardless of whether it maximally rewards or is of interest to the attorney.

3.2 DEVELOPING TRUST AND GOOD WORKING RELATIONSHIPS WITH CLIENTS

Let's summarize some of the key points of the text so far about legal interviewing in general and the initial client interview in particular. First, start the interview with open-ended questions and allow the client to state what happened in an uninterrupted fashion. Second, formulate probing questions which provide the details necessary to evaluate possibly relevant legal claims or defenses. Combine open and probing questions to explore each topic relevant to the legal analysis in the case. Third, identify the client's goals for the representation at some point in the interview. Fourth, listen in an engaged manner throughout the interview to build rapport and trust with the client.

This last point broaches a broader subject that is worth a bit more detail. One of the most important objectives in a client interview is to begin to establish a relationship of trust with the client. This section notes briefly the importance of trust in the client relationship and some ways to help build trust with the client.

3.2.1 TRUST-BUILDING

Establishing rapport in an interview will help promote trust with the client. *See* Section 2.5. In some client interview situations, the client will not feel permission to share embarrassing or difficult information in response to direct questions by an attorney who has not earned the client's trust. The trust and rapport you build in your interactions with the client will be critical later in the relationship when the pressure likely builds for all people involved in the case. Think ahead to the mediation simulation and working with your client to develop a negotiating plan in that environment.   You want your client to feel comfortable talking with you and confident in your commitment to achieving the client's goals.

A good way to build rapport is to ask the client about themselves. The level of detail will depend on the context of the representation. Asking about the client's work typically is appropriate whenever an individual client has a job. Most clients, like most of us in almost any role, like to talk about themselves. It helps the client feel heard.

The concept of trust-building as a cornerstone of positive and collaborative relationships with clients cuts across professions.   In medicine, as in law, "it is essential for patients to believe that their physicians are their agents and will represent their interests effectively."[2] Studies show that schools work most effectively when principals trust teachers and teachers trust parents.[3]

3.2.2   COMPLETING THE INTERVIEW

Building trust with the client is part of the larger concern of developing a positive working relationship with your client.   The conclusion of the interview provides another opportunity to build a good working relationship by providing clear guidance on the representation process. Conclude the interview by letting the client know the steps that will be taken and what the attorney expects from the client. For instance, if the client promised to provide documents, agree on a timeline for this task.

The attorney also can use the conclusion of the interview to summarize important information shared by the client during the interview. Stating the attorney's understanding of the client's goals verifies to the client that the attorney understand his priorities for the representation and was listening to him. The same can be said of repeating back the key facts stated by the client.

3.3 CLIENT DIVERSITY

We have so far presented a generic concept of "the client." The practice of law can vary depending on the type of clients the attorney represents. This section briefly introduces three types of client diversity: cultural differences, organizational clients and public agencies. Understanding client diversity is critical to effectively representing clients because

---

[2] David Mechanic, *The Functions and Limitations of Trust in the Provision of Medical Care*, 23 J. HEALTH POL. POL'Y & L. 661, 666–67 (1998). *See also* WILLIAM M. SULLIVAN ET AL., EDUCATING LAWYERS: PREPARATION FOR THE PROFESSION OF LAW 130 (2007)("Training in how to establish and maintain trust in the relationship with one's patients is addressed at many points in medical education.").

[3] Roger D. Goddard et al., *A Multilevel Examination of the Distribution and Effects of Teacher Turst in Students and Parents in Urban Elementary Schools*, ELEMENTARY SCH. J. 3 (2001); Megan Tschannen-Moran & Wayne K. Hoy, *A Multidisciplinary Analysis of the Nature, Meaning, and Measurement of Trust*, 70 REV. EDUC. RES. 547 (2000).

different clients demand the exercise of different skills and sets of knowledge to maintain properly the attorney-client relationship.

3.3.1 MULTICULTURAL FLUENCY

Anne Fadiman tells the story of a recently arrived Hmong immigrant family living in Fremont, California in the early 1980s.[4] A daughter in this family had epilepsy and the family sought treatment for her from two local pediatricians, Neil Ernst and Peggy Philip. Fadiman describes Dr. Ernst and Dr. Phillip as well-educated, smart, compassionate and hard-working—the type of doctor most of us would seek out when possible. These doctors prescribed treatment for the child that would keep her alive and healthy, but the child ultimately died because the doctors and the Hmong family were unable to effectively communicate and develop a relationship of trust. Fadiman concludes, "I have come to believe that her life was ruined...by cross-cultural misunderstanding."[5]

Few students enter law school today with no exposure to the concept of communicating across different cultures. Yet most students are not prepared to represent effectively a client from a wholly different background and experience. Attorneys can fail to help a client despite adequate or even exemplary legal research and analysis due to failure to communicate with a client who has a different cultural framework for sharing information or interpreting the meaning of information.[6] Professor Susan Bryant observes that, "[t]he capacity to form trusting relationships, to evaluate credibility, to develop client-centered case strategies and solutions, to gather information and to attribute the intended meaning from behavior and expressions are all affected by cultural experiences."[7]

As with Dr. Ernst and Dr. Phillip, developing cultural competence can have a life or death consequence in the law. Attorneys with the Gulf Region Advocacy Center represent foreign nationals facing the death penalty. Attorneys from this organization advise that, "[u]pon enrolling to represent a foreign national, the defense team should immediately begin a crash course in the history, geography, local culture and customs, politics, religion, medical practices, and infrastructure of a client's country of origin. Start with books and movies and then reach out to members of that community who live in the United States."[8] This advice

---

[4] ANNE FADIMAN, THE SPIRIT CATCHES YOU AND YOU FALL DOWN: A HMONG CHILD, HER AMERICAN DOCTORS, AND THE COLLISION OF TWO CULTURES (1997).

[5] *Id.* at 262.

[6] *See generally* Paul R. Tremblay, *Interviewing and Counseling Across Cultures: Heuristics and Biases,* 9 CLINICAL L REV. 373 (2002).

[7] Susan Bryant, *The Five Habits: Building Cross-Cultural Competence in Lawyers,* 8 CLINICAL L REV. 33, 42–43 (2001).

[8] Danalynn Recer, et al., *Representing Foreign National Capital Defendants,* 42 U. MEM. L. REV. 965 (2012).

results from these attorneys' understanding that "[a] capital client's culture impacts every aspect of the case."[9]

3.3.2   ORGANIZATIONAL CLIENTS

What do you think of when you hear the word "client"? You may have an image of someone dressed in jeans or someone dressed in business attire or something entirely different, but the common denominator usually is that your client is an individual person. In fact, most attorneys represent organizations, including businesses, nonprofit corporations, and a variety of other entities, rather than individuals.[10]

The organization will interact with the attorney through individual people, of course, but the attorney's client is the organization. Ethical rules make this clear.[11] The attorney takes direction from authorized officials or agents of the corporation, but it is important to remember that the client is the organization, not the individuals who hire the attorney and direct her work.[12]

Various types of organizational clients demand varying approaches to the attorney-client relationship. Nowecki Dry Cleaner is an organizational client, but so is ExxonMobil Corporation. The market for legal services to the largest corporate clients has gone through rapid changes. A generation ago it was common for large corporations to give one law firm primary responsibility for providing outside legal services. Today, legal work for these companies can be broken up into pieces and each project evaluated to match legal services to the highest value provider of those services, whether that means engaging a large law firm, contracting with a company that performs specific tasks through outsourcing the work to another country with lower costs, or other forms of providing legal services.[13]

Attorneys should strive to develop a trusting relationship with the client. Yet the meaning of trust, as with other aspects of the attorney-client relationship, will as a practical matter depend on the context of the representation, including the nature of the client and the work performed.

---

[9] *Id.* at 982.

[10] John P. Heinz, et. al., *The Changing Character of Lawyer's Work: Chicago in 1975 and 1995,* 32 Law & Soc'y Rev. 751 (1998).

[11] Model Rules of Prof'l Conduct R. 1.13(a) (2012).

[12] Ethical issues result when individual officers of the corporation direct the attorney to take actions not consistent with the interests of the organization. *See* Roger C. Cramton, *Counseling Organizational Clients "Within The Bounds of the Law,"* 34 HOFSTRA L. REV. 1043 (2006).

[13] *See* Steven A. Lauer, *The Development of the Corporate Law Department and Its Consequences,* OF COUNSEL, December 2010, at 6 (discussing the history of and modern unbundling of corporate legal services). More generally, attorneys providing legal services for large corporations increasingly face various pressures that were not present in past generations, including the need to reduce costs, provide global services and integrate advanced technology in service provision.

3.3.3   PUBLIC ATTORNEYS

Representing public entities deserve special mention.   A substantial portion of the profession, about 18%, is employed by government.[14]

The client relationship usually takes a different form with government attorneys.   Some attorneys work for the government but have a client relationship governed by the same principles as private sector attorneys; public defenders, for instance.   Many government attorneys have a client but also have obligations to the general public that extend beyond the interests of the client, such as an attorney in a state Attorney General's Office who represents the state Department of Education.   Other public attorneys, such as criminal prosecutors or regulators with civil enforcement authority, do not have a traditional client, but rather have obligations to the public at large.[15]

---

[14] U.S. DEPARTMENT OF LABOR, BUREAU OF LABOR STATISTICS, OCCUPATIONAL OUTLOOK HANDBOOK (2010), *available at* http://www.bls.gov/ooh/legal/lawyers.htm#tab-3.

[15] J. Nick Badgerow, *Walking the Line: Government Lawyer Ethics*, KAN. J.L. & PUB. POL'Y, Spring 2003, at 437.

CHAPTER 4

VOLUNTARY WITNESS INTERVIEWS

■ ■ ■

This chapter examines how attorneys conduct interviews of a witness or potential witness.[1] The primary objective in a witness interview usually is the acquisition of information. The attorney wants to know what the witness knows—about observed events, about other possible avenues of investigation, or any other useful knowledge held by the witness. The accuracy of the information that the attorney receives in the interview will be limited by the accuracy of the witness's memory and by the willingness of the witness to share that information.

Section 4.1 explores interviewing techniques that can enhance witness memory and disclosure. Section 4.2 looks at factors that impact witness cooperation, including whether or not the witness is favorably disposed to the interviewing attorney's client. Section 4.3 shifts the focus from assisting witness recall to the ethical and professional concerns raised by attorney interviews of witnesses. Finally, section 4.4 briefly notes purposes other than information acquisition during a witness interview.

4.1 PROMOTING WITNESS DISCLOSURE

This section elaborates on the fundamental interviewing techniques previously presented by discussing other interviewing techniques and methods to increase the amount of accurate information provided in a witness interview.

4.1.1   MEMORY FORMATION

An interview is a formal conversation with the primary purpose of probing the memory of the interviewee. Human memory is not like electronic memory. An obvious difference is that people forget information, starting with the moment an event or series of events are observed by or participated in by the interviewee.

---

[1] This chapter uses the term "witness" to mean a person other than the client of the attorney. In practice, the attorney may want to talk to people who are not "witnesses" in that they will never be called to testify at trial or in a deposition. For instance, the attorney may want to interview someone with experience in a particular industry who knows of the type of information that an opposing party is likely to have available in discovery but who neither has personal knowledge as to the records maintained by the opposing party nor would qualify as an expert.

More fundamentally, psychological researchers have developed a model of human memory that suggests memory is less an imperfect imprinting of reality, and more like a re-mixing of actual and imagined details influenced by biases, self-interest and later events. Psychologists John Turtle and Stephen Want have described memory as "a reconstructive process, inherently prone to errors of commission and omission."[2] People "remember" events that never occurred in their lives.[3] College students asked to recall high school grades consistently overestimate their grade point average.[4]

Understanding that memory formation is not a matter of simple recall has numerous implications for the attorney interviewing process. As noted in Section 2.3.2, novice attorneys have a tendency to accept statements by an interviewee as an accurate recounting of events. The reconstructive nature of memory means that testimony by multiple witnesses about an event can conflict even when the witnesses believe they are accurately recounting observations. It is critical for the attorney conducting an interview not to make assumptions about what can be known definitively given a narrow set of interview data.

The interviewing techniques in Chapters 2 and 3 are based in part on the nature of memory and recall. Using open-end questions followed by probing questions maximizes different types of human recall and together these questions types are thought to produce both the highest quantity and most accurate information.[5] The next two subsections examine other questioning methods that can be useful for promoting information disclosure by witnesses.

---

[2] John Turtle & Stephen C. Want, *Logic and Research Versus Intuition and Past Practice as Guides to Gathering and Evaluating Eyewitness Evidence*, 35 CRIM. JUST. & BEHAV. 1241, 1244 (2008).

[3] D. Stephen Lindsay, et al., *True Photographs and False Memories*, 15 PSYCHOL. SCI. 149, 153 (2004) (finding that two-thirds of subjects reported false memory when shown an old school photograph and asked about both real experiences and events invented by the researchers). Professor Elizabeth Loftus, who studies false memory formation, summarized decades of research in the field as follows: "[Distortion in memory] has been found in hundreds of studies involving a wide variety of materials. People have recalled nonexistent objects such as broken glass. They have been misled into remembering a yield sign as a stop sign, hammers as screwdrivers, and even something large, like a barn, that was not part of the bucolic landscape by which an automobile happened to be driving. Details have been planted into memory for simulated events that were witnessed (e.g. a filmed accident), but also into memory for real-world events such as the planting of wounded animals (that were not seen) into memory for the scene of a tragic terrorist bombing that actually had occurred in Russia a few years earlier." Elizabeth F. Loftus, *Planting Misinformation in the Human Mind: A 30-Year Investigation of the Malleability of* Memory, 12 LEARNING & MEMORY 361, 361 (2005).

[4] Harry P. Bahrick, et al., *Accuracy and Distortion in Memory for High School Grades*, 7 PSYCHOL.SCI.,265 (1996). These researchers observed that the students showed "a strong tendency to generate emotionally gratifying content [higher grades]."

[5] *See* Lauren R. Shapiro, *The Effects of Question Type and Eyewitness Temperament on Accuracy and Quantity of*

Recall for a Simulated Misdemeanor Crime, 43 EMPORIA ST. RES. SERIES 1 (2006) (summarizing and extending research on the impact of open-end or closed-end questioning in witness recall).

4.1.2   MEMORY PROBING TECHNIQUES

A series of techniques known as "cognitive interviewing" was developed in the mid-1980s to aid police in crime investigation.[6]   The cognitive interview method has repeatedly been shown in both laboratory and field settings to be effective in promoting accurate witness recall.[7]   In addition to encouraging a narrative phase of the interview with active listening and questioning of the type described here as "open-probe," the cognitive interview suggests interviewers use the following mnemonics:

(1) *Try to get the interviewee to reinstate the context.*   In the situation of a police or accident investigation, the interviewer should attempt to have the witness try to recreate the physical environment in which the event occurred.   Cognitive interviewing encourages bringing the witness back to the location of the event, if possible.   Or try to have the witness recreate the environment in which statements or decisions were made, business was conducted or the like.   For example, ask a witness in a sexual harassment case to describe the office environment and the people involved.   Try to get the witness to recreate the image of the environment in her mind.

(2) *Encourage the interviewee to report everything.*   Cognitive interview technique includes instruction (repeated more than once during the interview) to the interviewee to tell everything that she can remember, even if it seems irrelevant.   This instruction serves two purposes—to prevent self-censorship as much as possible and to create multiple paths of recall so that the witness's recall of particular events triggers memory of other relevant matters.

(3) *Ask the interviewee to recount the events in a variety of orders or perspectives.* This mnemonic is based on the understanding that memory is stored in the human mind in a variety of ways so that its retrieval can be aided by getting the witness to approach recall from different viewpoints.   Chronological order is an easy way to organize events, but also try to ask questions that require the witness to reconstruct events at different points in the time sequence.   Or ask the witness to describe events through the perspective of others involved in the matter.   Similarly, it can be effective in some contexts to have the witness use non-verbal recall, such as drawing a map or re-enacting movements.[8]

---

[6] Edward Geiselman, et al., *Enhancement of Eyewitness Memory: An Empirical Evaluation of the Cognitive Interview,* 12 J. POLICE SCI. & ADMIN. 74 (1984).

[7] Brian R. Clifford & Richard George, *A Field Evaluation of Training in Three Methods of Witness/Victim Investigative Interviewing,* 2 PSYCHOL., CRIME & L. 231 (1996); Robyn E. Holliday, et al., *The Cognitive Interview: Research and Practice Across the Lifespan, in* HANDBOOK OF PSYCHOLOGY OF INVESTIGATIVE INTERVIEWING 137 (Ray Bull et al. eds. 2009) (observing that cognitive interview techniques have been shown effective in more than 100 studies in the United States, United Kingdom, Australia, and Germany).

[8] Eric Shepherd & Rebecca Milne, *'Have You Told Management About This?': Bringing Witness Interviewing Into the Twenty-First Century, in,* WITNESS TESTIMONY: PSYCHOLOGICAL,

4.1.3   PROBING SOURCES OF KNOWLEDGE

Imagine that you represent a government environmental protection agency. You are engaged in a dispute with a trucking company related to ground water pollution caused by leakage of petroleum from old underground storage tanks at the company's site. Your agency maintains that the company knew about the leak but failed to report it for at least two years prior to the agency's discovery of the problem. The company claims it just learned about the problem the week before the agency discovered the contamination. There is a substantial difference in possible penalties and sanctions if the company was aware of the problem for two years versus knew of the leak just one week prior to agency knowledge.

The company's site is located next to a housing development that was built four years prior to agency discovery of the contamination. You interview one of the homeowners in that development who tells you that he knows about the contamination. You engage in the following exchange with this homeowner:

> Attorney: When you did first learn that your groundwater was contaminated?
>
> Homeowner: At least a year ago. Maybe longer.
>
> Attorney: Do you know if your neighbors also were aware of the contamination a year ago?
>
> Homeowner: We all pretty much knew there was a problem. Norm and Judy Bassett across the street were talking about it with me when they put their house on the market last year. They were saying that their realtor told them they probably should disclose there may be a groundwater problem when they filled out their selling papers. So we all have known for awhile now.

What else should you inquire about with this homeowner? One of the most important probing questions you will want to ask this homeowner is how he acquired knowledge of the groundwater contamination. If he responds, for instance, that he knew about the contamination because "you could kind of smell it after a really hard rain," that is useful information for your case. If he responds that "you just have to assume that's what it will be when you live next to a place that is constantly fueling up big trucks," that is less helpful for proving your case. But if the homeowner tells you, "a family over on Sycamore found out two years ago when they went to build an addition and the contractor had to stop

---

INVESTIGATIVE AND EVIDENTIAL PERSPECTIVES 140–42 (Anthony Heaton-Armstrong et al. eds. 2006). Notice how Mr. Orfield uses a map to better convey his experience with Officer Feldman in the the initial video.

and do some tests because they got a gas smell when they began moving earth," you have opened up a potentially very productive route for further investigation.

A critical part of most interviews is discovering not only what the person knows, but also how that person acquired the knowledge. Inquiring about the source of knowledge deepens understanding of the facts that witness can reveal. This type of inquiry also can lead to corroborating witnesses, documents or other sources of information.

Probing sources of knowledge also will be critical if the case proceeds from the initial fact gathering stage to motions and trial. A witness interview in a dispute resolution situation usually is a prelude to obtaining testimony from that witness or others. In other words, the attorney is gathering future evidence for a trial or to support motion briefing. The source of the witnesses' knowledge will be important to determining whether he can provide admissible evidence.

4.2 WITNESS COOPERATION

A primary difference between a witness interview and a client interview is that the witness may not want to help your client achieve his objectives. In fact, the witness may want to see the opposing party prevail in the dispute with your client. The disposition of the witness toward your client can substantially influence the form of the interview.

Commentators often divide witnesses into three types: friendly, neutral or adverse.[9] These categories have intuitively obvious meanings: friendly witnesses want to help your client; hostile witnesses want to help the opposing party, or at least do not want to see your client succeed; and neutral witnesses have no preference as to who prevails in the dispute. Witnesses actually may have complex motives or affiliations that cut across these categories, but these archetypes allow for useful generalizations about different interviewing techniques.

4.2.1 NEUTRAL WITNESSES

The attorney usually can plan interview questions for a neutral witness consistent with the open-probe method and other fundamental interviewing techniques elaborated in Chapter 2. A key to a neutral witness interview is to build and maintain a positive relationship. If the

---

[9] *See, e.g.*, ROGER S. HAYDOCK, ET AL., FUNDAMENTALS OF PRETRIAL LITIGATION 65 (8th ed. 2011). The disposition of the witness is a different concern than whether the information possessed by the witness is useful or adverse to your client's case. A hostile witness may share information that is the missing ingredient in proving a claim. Or a friendly witness may have knowledge that would destroy an otherwise viable defense. The disposition of the witness speaks to that person's motive and bias for or against your client, not necessarily whether that person will aid or damage your case.

witness provides relevant information about an issue in dispute, the attorney may encounter that witness again in follow-up interviews or at a deposition or trial. Building trust with neutral witnesses pays off through the course of lengthy litigation. Active listening, integrity in responding to witness concerns, and a reasonable and cooperative manner can make a difference in obtaining the most favorable witness testimony consistent with the witness's recall.

Trust-building also can mean better access to the witness. While a neutral witness may not be opposed to seeing your client succeed in the dispute, that witness may be more or less inclined to spend the time to tell you about their observations, or to provide depth about topics of interest to the interviewing attorney. An uninvolved observer of an accident or event may have little reason to engage in a lengthy discussion with an interviewing attorney, especially if that witness considers the potential of much more time disappearing when subpoenaed for testimony in the case. And if the witness provides favorable information for the attorney's client, the attorney may want to obtain testimony from that witness in a less costly and more certain manner via a voluntary affidavit rather than a compelled deposition, which is not very likely if the witness is annoyed by or mistrusts the attorney. A cooperative and approachable demeanor can only be an asset with respect to your access to and cooperation by the witness.

4.2.2   HOSTILE WITNESSES

Potentially hostile witnesses willing to talk with the attorney representing the disfavored party present a more difficult interview challenge[10]. The first challenge is deciding whether the witness is actually hostile. A presumptively hostile witness may have a different disposition when interviewed, or a presumptively friendly witness may be problematic. For example, you may find a hostile witness whom your client led you to believe would be cooperative. Or the witness may have surprising motives, such as discovering that a close relative of the opposing party actually has a long-standing grudge against that person. Start the interview by evaluating whether the witness is properly considered hostile. Engaging the witness in "small talk" or asking one open-ended question about the matter may prompt a declaration or clear message of the person's disposition toward your client.

Approaching a hostile witness with open-end questions rarely succeeds because she is unlikely to provide much of a response. Open-end

---

[10] Even when hostile witnesses are willing to talk with the attorney, attorneys with the resources available to hire an investigator usually have the investigator conduct the interview. If the attorney performs the interview and later wants to use statements made in the interview to impeach the credibility of a witness who presents a contrary version of the facts when testifying, the attorney could be disqualified from representing the client because he could become a fact witness.

questions and responses may be a trust-building process, but participating with the interviewee in this process usually requires a willingness to positively engage with the interviewer. That is an initial level of trust that does not usually exist between the interviewing attorney and the hostile witness.

Consider inverting the order of question type with a hostile witness. In other words, use a probe-open method. Start by inquiring about specific facts. Make the witness be clear about the exact details that he knows, so that you are aware of the specific testimony that he may later provide in the case. You also can ask direct questions about other witnesses, sources of evidence or the like because open-end questions at the beginning of the interview are unlikely to elicit this sort of data.

After you have engaged the hostile witness with as many relevant probing questions for which you can obtain an answer, the tenor of the discussion may have shifted. This is especially true if you have practiced active listening techniques and generally been attentive to the witness. At this point in the interview, you can try introducing open-end questions. Don't underestimate the power of positive human interaction to create trust, or at least neutralize mistrust, during an interview. Of course, open-end questions may still be a futile effort even after a well-conducted interview.

4.3 ETHICAL WITNESS INTERVIEWS

This section briefly addresses two professional responsibility rules concerning contacts by attorneys with non-clients.

4.3.1　ETHICAL REQUIREMENTS FOR ALL WITNESS INTERVIEWS

The Model Rules of Professional Conduct contain two rules that directly relate to the task of interviewing people other than the attorney's client. Rule 4.2 prohibits direct contact with people who are represented by counsel.[11] When the attorney knows that the person is represented by counsel in the matter at issue, the attorney must contact that counsel. The attorney may interview the person only if that person's counsel consents. The attorney must have actual knowledge that the person is represented for Rule 4.2 to apply. It is not usually required for the attorney to inquire if the person is represented but the attorney "cannot

---

[11] MODEL RULES OF PROF'L CONDUCT R. 4.2 states: "In representing a client, a lawyer shall not communicate about the subject of the representation with a person the lawyer knows to be represented by another lawyer in the matter, unless the lawyer has the consent of the other lawyer or is authorized to do so by law or a court order."

evade the requirement" of Rule 4.2 by "closing eyes to the obvious" when representation can be inferred from the circumstances.[12]

When the non-client being interviewed is not represented by counsel, Rule 4.3 imposes obligations on attorneys.[13] The attorney must avoid giving legal advice to the interviewee other than the advice to obtain counsel when she "knows or reasonably should know" that her client's interests are or may become in conflict with the interests of the person being interviewed. In any circumstance, the interviewing attorney must be clear as to her role. The attorney cannot expressly or impliedly represent that she is a disinterested person. And the attorney has an affirmative obligation to correct a misimpression about her role if the attorney knows or reasonably should know that the interviewee misunderstands that role. It is good practice in most situations for an attorney to avoid this type of confusion by simply identifying her client and that she represents the client in the matter to be discussed.

4.3.2   INFLUENCING TESTIMONY AND OTHER ETHICAL CONCERNS

Some witness interviews require a special approach. As with all aspects of legal practice, the context of the legal practice will dictate much about whether special circumstances exist. For example, the difficult situation of interviewing children in family law and criminal sexual abuse cases implicates both practical and ethical questions about interview techniques.[14]

An ethical matter of more general concern in witness interviews is the question of when an attorney may be influencing witness testimony. If memory is a reconstruction of events, then perhaps the interviewing attorney can shape the interviewee's recall of the event. The ethical and professional dangers of this observation should be patent for any attorney or law student.

Think about the difference between attorneys attempting to influence recall of an event versus attorneys attempting to influence how a witness

---

12 Model Rules of Prof'l Conduct R. 4.2 cmt. 8.

13 Rule 4.3 states: "In dealing on behalf of a client with a person who is not represented by counsel, a lawyer shall not state or imply that the lawyer is disinterested. When the lawyer knows or reasonably should know that the unrepresented person misunderstands the lawyer's role in the matter, the lawyer shall make reasonable efforts to correct the misunderstanding. The lawyer shall not give legal advice to an unrepresented person, other than the advice to secure counsel, if the lawyer knows or reasonably should know that the interests of such a person are or have a reasonable possibility of being in conflict with the interests of the client." MODEL RULES OF PROF'L CONDUCT R. 4.3.

14   See, e.g., Karen Saywitz, et al., Interviewing Children in Child Custody Cases: Implications of Research and Policy for Practice 28 BEHAV. SCI. L. 542 (2010). See also Amina Memon, et al., A Field Evaluation of the VIPER System: A New Technique for Eliciting Eyewitness Identification Evidence, 17 PSYCHOL. L. & CRIME 711 (2011) (describing interviewing techniques to use with various vulnerable groups).

testifies about that recall. The latter problem is the focus of a great deal of scholarly and practitioner comment on the proper limits of preparing witnesses for impending testimony or of attorney attempts to "coach" witnesses before and during a deposition.[15]

The former problem—when can or should attorneys attempt in an interview to shape how a witness recalls events—more directly implicates the witness interview simulation. Obviously, an attorney should not (and ethically cannot) attempt to influence a witness to recall events falsely. It is improper to suggest to a friendly witness that a "yes" answer to an impending question would "be very helpful to your employer," or the like. The more difficult question is whether the attorney can or should attempt to influence testimony by asking questions during the interview that might impact how a witness recalls an event even though the attorney is not signaling to the witness how the attorney wants the witness to answer the question. For instance, if a witness expresses doubt, how should the attorney explore the extent and nature of that doubt, and in the process of asking those questions perhaps shape how the witness recalls the event? A thorough treatment of this issue is beyond the scope of this introductory text. For now, be alert to whether your witness interview simulation presents a situation in which you might have the opportunity for (and danger of) shaping witness recollection.

4.4 PURPOSES OF A WITNESS INTERVIEW

As stated at the beginning of this chapter, the primary purpose of a witness interview usually is to acquire specific information from the witness to help evaluate or strengthen claims and defenses. Other purposes exist for reaching out to witnesses.

Corroborate the Client's Story. It is not unusual for an attorney to hear about a situation from a client and then later discover that the client's story is fundamentally inaccurate or omits critical information. An important function of witness interviews, therefore, is to verify the accuracy and completeness of the information presented by the client. Witnesses can shed light not only the strength of possible claims or defenses, but also can help the attorney determine the degree to which his client is an accurate source of information and later credible testimony about the matter presented.

Confirming the client's story is especially valuable early in consideration of potential litigation. An attorney may have an obligation to search for information that corroborates or contradicts the information provided by the client. The court can impose sanctions if the attorney fails to make an

---

[15] *See, e.g.,* Bennett L. Gershman, *Witness Coaching by Prosecutors,* 23 CARDOZO L. REV. 829 (2002); A. Darby Dickerson, *The Law and Ethics of Civil Depositions,* 57 MD. L. REV. 273 (1998).

"inquiry reasonable under the circumstances" to determine if the facts alleged in the Complaint have evidentiary support.[16]

Determine Whether the Witness is Friendly, Neutral or Hostile. Section 4.2 notes that it is often not possible prior to the interview to classify a witness as friendly, neutral or hostile. One of the purposes of talking to witnesses is to find who wants to help or hurt the client in favorably resolving a dispute.

Evaluating Witness Demeanor. The word "witness" means someone who has knowledge of events or other facts, but it also means someone who provides testimony in a legal proceeding. Attorneys can use the witness interview process to make judgments about how that person likely will present herself under questioning at trial; judgments about the believability or persuasiveness of that person as a witness at trial.

---

[16] FED. R. CIV. P. 11.

CHAPTER 5

DEPOSITIONS: QUESTIONING WHEN MAKING A RECORD

■ ■ ■

A deposition is a formal, recorded and transcribed interview. This chapter introduces students to the basic skills needed to plan for and conduct a deposition.

Fact investigation by interviewing the client and witnesses allows the attorney to acquire information useful for evaluating claims and defenses. Trial testimony allows the attorney to use questioning as a means of eliciting statements that will persuade a decision-maker. A deposition can be conducted either for the purpose of acquiring information or to build a persuasive record that will be presented in court, or for both reasons. It is important for the attorney to identify the reasons for taking the deposition as part of preparing for the examination. Section 5.1 looks at common purposes for deposing a witness and how the attorney can prepare deposition questions and strategy to achieve those purposes.

When the attorney may want to use the transcribed deposition testimony in a court proceeding, either in support of a motion or at trial, questioning a witness at a deposition involves attention to how the questions and answers will appear in a written record. Section 5.2 examines the problem of constructing questions and obtaining responses so that the deposition record can be effectively used with the court or jury.

Many of the techniques used in witness interviews apply to deposition examination. Section 5.3 re-visits fundamental interview techniques in the context of a deposition, including asking probing questions in a formal setting. This section also examines the critical skill of listening for unexpected information and incorporating that information into the examination.

Finally, Section 5.4 reviews several practical matters to assist attorneys in their first deposition. This section describes the beginning and close of a deposition, the use of documents in the examination and objections by opposing counsel during a deposition.

5.1 DEPOSITION PURPOSE AND PLAN

Depositions cost money.   Each client paying an hourly fee will be billed for the time its attorney is at the deposition plus the attorney's preparation time.   And the client of the attorney who provided notice of the deposition will pay for the court reporter's time and fees.   Given the costs involved, attorneys using their power to force a witness to attend a deposition should have a clear idea of what can be achieved from the deposition and a strategy for how to obtain the desired result.   Then the attorney should carefully prepare to implement that strategy.

5.1.1   IDENTIFYING DEPOSITION PURPOSES

Attorneys compel deposition testimony for a variety of reasons.   Four of the most common, legitimate reasons for taking a deposition are described below.

   * *Acquiring Information.*   Depositions sometimes are used to obtain information that the attorney would rather obtain voluntarily but the deponent[1] will not discuss without being compelled to attend.   For example, a former litigant in a completed lawsuit may be subject to a confidentiality provision in a settlement agreement that prevents freely discussing her experience with others.   Or a deposition of an opposing party may be primarily for the purpose of acquiring information rather than forcing the opposing party to respond to questions for the purpose of making a record.   For instance, an attorney will sometimes issue a notice asking an opposing party to designate for deposition a person with knowledge of that party's data processing systems.[2]   The purpose of the deposition is to obtain information about the opposing party's data systems; information useful for constructing specific future discovery requests seeking electronically stored information.   The transcript may be used in a later discovery motion or for other purposes, but the attorney's primary purpose is to get detailed information as a building block for other discovery.

   * *Freezing Testimony.*   Depositions lay the groundwork for trial.[3]   It is difficult to prepare for cross-examination of a witness, such as the opposing party, whom you likely have had no opportunity to interview.   Even if the attorney has interviewed a witness, the witness may change his story at trial.   A deposition allows the attorney to "freeze" the story of

---

[1] The witness at a deposition is called the deponent.

[2] *See* FED. R. CIV. P. 30 (b)(6) (allowing a party to notice a deposition requiring the opposing party to designate a deponent with knowledge of identified matters).

[3] This section assumes that the attorney expects the witness to be available at trial. Another use of depositions is to preserve trial testimony for witnesses that are or may become unable or unwilling to testify at trial.   Examples of such witnesses are individuals who are beyond the subpoena power of the trial court, or individuals who are ill and may not be in sufficiently good health to testify at trial.

a possible trial witness by obtaining a written record of the deponent's responses at the deposition. The witness can deviate from his deposition response at trial, but the deposition testimony can be used to impeach that witness, thus casting doubt on his credibility.

   * *Obtaining Support for a Motion.* Deposition testimony often is a primary source of facts used by attorneys to support or oppose a motion, especially a summary judgment motion.[4] Deposition testimony of the opposing party usually is a more fruitful method of obtaining admissions than interrogatory answers or requests for admission because the attorney can ask repeated follow-up questions and the answer comes directly from the deponent, rather than in a written form likely drafted by the opposing counsel.

   * *Evaluating Deponent Demeanor.* A deposition is an excellent opportunity to see how a witness behaves and appears under formal questioning. In some cases, evaluating deponent demeanor can be the primary or even sole purpose for taking the deposition. For example, if the case turns on the credibility of two opposing individual parties with already known contradictory recollections of an event, an attorney may take a deposition to see how the unfavorable witness will appear on the witness stand. The attorney might use this information to determine the settlement value of the case, as well as for trial preparation.

5.1.2   DEPOSITION PREPARATION FOLLOWS PURPOSE

After determining the purpose of the deposition, the attorney should prepare a strategy for inquiry designed to achieve that purpose for the deposition.

Depositions to *acquire information* can proceed mostly as would occur in a witness interview, as explored in Chapters 2 and 4, developing topics to be explored through use of the open-probe method with modification for witnesses that are hostile.

Preparation by attorneys seeking to *freeze the deponent's testimony* should start from the likely testimony of the witness. Why will this witness testimony be presented by one side or the other at trial? The attorney should consider all the testimony that this witness may be able to offer at trial and create an outline for the deposition that will cover all of these topics. Questioning for this type of deposition should rely heavily on the skills of asking detailed probing questions (*see* Sections 2.2.2 and 5.3.1) and questioning that will create a clear written record (*see* Section 5.2).

---

[4] The other sources of factual support for a motion include testimony in affidavits, documents, and interrogatory answers or responses to requests for admission. *See, e.g.*, FED. R. CIV. P. 56(c)(1)(A) (listing sources of factual support for a summary judgment motion).

Similarly, attorneys seeking to *gain support for a motion* should initially identify the facts relevant to the elements of proof at issue in the motion. This type of deposition requires the attorney to be precise about the factual support needed for each element of the claims or defenses. It is critical that the attorney make sure that the recorded responses of the deponent make a clear written record that can be used in support of the motion (*see* Section 5.2). The attorney should identify the exact admission or testimony that will best prove or disprove each element. Once useful testimony is obtained on a particular point, the attorney can do damage by continuing to examine the deponent in this type of deposition and perhaps creating ambiguity as to the deponent's testimony.

Depositions taken for the primary purpose of *evaluating deponent demeanor* suggests preparation different than the above approaches. Deposition transcripts for motion support and freezing testimony are used in nuggets—excerpts that provide support for a particular point or contradict later testimony on a particular subject. Evaluating witness demeanor can be based on information that may not even appear in the transcript of the deposition. The deponent may appear arrogant or evasive in person when the written record would suggest neither observation. Questioning for evaluating demeanor should involve varying styles to see how the deponent reacts to different types of questions.

5.1.3   MULTIPLE OR SHIFTING DEPOSITION PURPOSES

In practice, the purpose of the deposition usually will not be so clearly defined to one of the above categories. Depositions frequently will be taken for multiple purposes. The deposing attorney may want motion support and information and observation of demeanor. The purpose of the deposition also may be murky because the attorney is wholly unsure of what the witness may know. Or the purpose of the deposition may change when the attorney carefully listens to the deponent's testimony.

It is nonetheless constructive for the attorney to identify and even prioritize deposition purposes when preparing for the examination. Most depositions will have one or two purposes that are more salient. Preparing for the deposition by reflecting on each purpose for which it can be used focuses the attorney's attention on different information and questioning strategies that may be prove useful.

5.2 MAKING A RECORD

Like trial testimony, deposition inquiry results in a formal record. Clarity of record is essential in depositions taken for the purposes of freezing witness testimony or gaining support for a motion. The need to effectively control the record makes deposition inquiry even less like casual conversation than a client or witness interview. Creating a usable record requires that the attorney ask clear questions and persist in obtaining clear answers.

5.2.1   CLEAR QUESTIONS

In everyday discussion we usually assume people involved in our conversations share an interest in mutual understanding and agreement. This assumption allows us to ask questions and exchange information efficiently based on context. A person might ask her colleague during the workday, "Are you going to stop by the bar later?" It would be unlikely that the colleague would respond by asking, "What do you mean by 'the bar'?" or, "By 'later' do you mean after work, later this week or some other time period?" The context of the discussion provides a common understanding as to the assumed place and time for the people involved in the conversation.

Attorneys in a deposition need to employ more formal, literal language. A deposition of an opposing party typically involves a conversation in which a desire for mutual understanding and agreement cannot be assumed. Even with a neutral deponent, the attorney is striving for something different than the meaning conveyed in casual conversation. The attorney is seeking an unambiguous record of the information conveyed by the deponent.

Consider as an example the following excerpt from a deposition of Ms. McDonald by counsel for Bi-Tell in the toxic gas case discussed in Section 2.1.

> Question: What symptoms did you notice when you first starting feeling ill during the morning of April 12, 2013?
>
> Answer: I started rubbing my eyes because they were itching. My nose started running. It was all really sudden.
>
> Question: Eye irritation and nasal discharge were your only symptoms?
>
> Answer: Yes.
>
> Question: And then you called your primary care doctor?
>
> Answer: Yes. I asked them right away about why I would suddenly start feeling bad.

What evidence has the attorney established in this deposition excerpt? Stop reading and write down what you think the attorney can assert in a summary judgment motion as proven by this record. Also note how you would rephrase or follow-up some or all of these questions to create as clear a record as possible.

The first question and answer make a sufficient record on at least two of Ms. McDonald's initial symptoms, although the order of the plaintiff's awareness of the two symptoms is unclear. One probably can conclude from the latter two questions and answers that Ms. McDonald had no symptoms from the toxic gas exposure other than itching eyes and a running nose, and that Ms. McDonald promptly called her doctor based on those two symptoms. Yet the latter two questions and responses lack the clarity needed to create a record that definitively proves these facts.

The latter two questions are ambiguous at least as to time. Perhaps Ms. McDonald was replying to the predicate of the initial question in her answer to the later questions; in other words, she was answering only about her symptoms when she "first starting feeling ill." Assume she developed shortness of breath a half hour after experiencing her initial symptoms. Ms. McDonald's answers to the latter two questions are consistent with her having later experienced breathing problems.

The attorney could have asked the question unambiguously in a number of ways. For example, the attorney could have inquired, "Did you experience any other symptoms prior to calling your doctor's office?" Depending on Ms. McDonald's responses, the attorney could ask follow-up questions to probe all the details of these symptoms using the familiar interrogatory questions. The attorney presumably would have the medical report created when Ms. McDonald arrived for treatment, which would provide a source for further inquiry about her initial symptoms.

This picayune analysis may seem unnatural, but learning to ask questions that are precise and unambiguous is a key skill for any litigator, and also is a trait that is of importance for attorneys working on transactional matters. Asking questions that make an effective record requires forming inquiries that convey all the information needed to unambiguously answer the question. This means the attorney needs to state expressly the predicate to the question.

Assumptions imbedded in a question are a common source of question ambiguity. The assumptions can be about knowledge of the matter at issue. For instance, in the above example the attorney asks Ms. McDonald about calling her "primary care doctor." Unless the record has been clearly established on this point, the attorney and the deponent may have a different understanding of who is Ms. McDonald's primary care doctor. It would be simple and clearer to just ask if Ms McDonald called the offices of Dr. X and to ask with whom she spoke.

Or the assumption can be based on prior questions asked by the attorney. The above example about eye irritation and nasal discharge as Ms. McDonald's only symptoms was ambiguous because it is unclear whether the predicate temporal reference in the prior question (when the deponent "first starting feeling ill") was incorporated in the next question. If so,

Ms. McDonald's answer means that eye irritation and nasal discharge were her only initial symptoms, not her only symptoms.

Pay particular attention to the use of pronouns in asking questions. Ambiguous questions often occur when the attorney uses pronouns like "he," "that" and "those" in reference to information elicited in prior questions. It is easy to assume at the moment of questioning that everyone knows what you mean, yet the cold reality of the written record read months or even years later will not necessarily support that assumption. Include express references to people, places or things when forming deposition questions.

5.2.2   PERSISTING TO A CLEAR RESPONSE

An ambiguous record also can occur with perfectly clear questions that the deponent fails to answer, whether purposefully or unintentionally. Hostile deponents may try to evade questions and provide answers that create ambiguity. Bill Clinton was clearly hostile when deposed while he was President of the United States about his sexual relationship with intern Monica Lewinski. He famously answered one question by stating, "It depends on what the meaning of the word 'is' is. If the—if he—if 'is' means is and never has been, that is not—that is one thing. If it means there is none, that was a completely true statement."[5]

Deponents also can give unclear answers without intent to evade the question. In some cases, the deponent may not know the answer to the question and just starts to talk around the question as a means of trying to convey information. Sometimes the deponent misconstrues a perfectly clear question. Non-responsive answers can happen in many ways and for many reasons.

Imagine that Ms. Cabot observed a car accident. She did not know anyone involved in the accident and is a neutral deponent. Her deposition included the following exchange:

> Question: Did you see how many people were in the black car when it collided with the red car?
>
> Answer: Yes.
>
> Question: How many people were in the black car when it collided with the red car?
>
> Answer: After the black car was hit and went up on the curb, I saw two people sort of jump out of it. There was a woman about 40 years old and a boy who looked to be in his early teens. Maybe he was older, like 18 years old or so.

---

[5]   KENNETH STARR, THE STARR REPORT: THE OFFICIAL REPORT OF THE INDEPENDENT COUNSEL'S INVESTIGATION OF THE PRESIDENT 212 n.1128 (1998).

Ms. Cabot's answer to the second question is ambiguous. It is clear from the answer that she saw two people get out of the car. It is not certain that Ms. Cabot saw only those two people in the car or that she saw those two people at the time of the collision. In response to the first question, perhaps she meant that she saw people get out of the black car and assumed those were the only people in the car, or perhaps she meant she saw inside the car and there were only those two people. Or Ms. Cabot could have seen three people and got lost telling the story about the two people jumping out of the car and their ages, and then just forgot to mention the third person.

Whatever Ms. Cabot saw, it is the job of the deposing attorney to pose follow-up questions that eliminate doubt about the deponent's observation of the number of people in the car at the time of the collision. A follow-up examination to obtain a clear response to the question asked could proceed as follows:

> Question: Did you see anyone else in the black car other than the two people you just described who jumped out of the car?
>
> Answer: No.
>
> Question: When did you first see that there were two people in the black car?
>
> Answer: When I saw them jump out.
>
> Question: So at the moment of the collision you did not know how many people were in the black car?
>
> Answer: That's right.
>
> Question: At the time the cars collided, did you see the person driving the black car?
>
> Answer: No. I first saw the people in that car when they jumped out.

Now the attorney has a clear answer to Ms. Cabot's knowledge of the people in the car at the moment of the collision. The attorney also knows that Ms. Cabot saw only two people jump out of the car after it went over the curb.

5.3 INTERVIEW TECHNIQUES REVISITED FOR DEPOSITIONS

Effective techniques for conducting a deposition also draw on the same fundamental interviewing skills elaborated in Chapters 2 through 4. This section applies some of those key concepts to the context of the deposition. This section also introduces the problem of how to examine a witness when unexpected information is disclosed.

5.3.1   PROBING QUESTIONING

After obtaining a clear response to the question posed to Ms. Cabot in the above example, do we know how many people were in the black car at the time of the collision? Not necessarily. We don't even know that Ms. Cabot saw only two people who had been in the black car. It is entirely possible that Ms. Cabot observed the cars collide and watched two people jump out of the black car, then turned her attention to calling for emergency help. Perhaps a third, injured man later emerged from the black car and lay down on the ground near the red car and Ms. Cabot talked to him, but she never saw him get out of the car and assumed he was riding in the red car.

The attorney who obtains the full knowledge of the deponent usually is the attorney who asks probing questions. As authors of a book on effective deposition techniques state, "You want details. If the witness is friendly, you want details because it helps the deponent tell a persuasive story. If the witness is hostile, you want details (often, but not necessarily always) to test credibility and to avoid later surprise."[6]

The process of making a record in a deposition requires more careful probing questions than is necessary, or even useful, in most initial client interviews. As discussed above, deposition questions have to be unambiguous and answers responsive when your purpose is to make a written record.

Depositions also differ from a client or witness interview because the attorney has one opportunity to ask questions of the deponent.[7] The attorney must be prepared to inquire about priority matters at the deposition. Failure to ask detailed deposition questions on a critical point can substantially hamper the evidence submitted with a summary judgment brief. Cases have been lost on dispositive motion because the attorney failed to inquire about the opposing party's knowledge of a particular fact. Lack of probing questions also can complicate the attorney's preparation for handling a witness at trial.

The open-probe method usually will provide a fruitful approach for asking questions in a deposition. If the witness is willing to provide narrative responses to open-end questions that broach a topic, the attorney should let the witness volunteer information. Of course, depositions often involve the opposing party or another hostile deponent. Well-coached hostile deponents are not likely to offer long narrative answers because the opposing counsel will have taught the deponent to answer only the questions asked. Hostile witnesses also can evade, distract or attack the

---

[6] Bradley G. Clary, et al., Successful First Depositions 48 (3d ed.)

[7] See Fed. R. Civ. P. 30 (a)(2)(A)(ii) (requiring leave of court to depose a person who has already given a deposition in the case).

deposing attorney, which presents a set of challenges beyond the scope of your assignment.[8]

Finally, probing questions at a deposition should include an exploration of the source of knowledge of the deponent. You want to know not only what the deponent knows, but also how the deponent acquired that information. For instance, a deponent in a case about misleading anti-trust violations may testify that a corporate officer was out of town at the time a critical meeting occurred. The attorney should probe the deponent as to how he allegedly knew that the officer was out of town. Consider the following testimony on the topic:

> Answer: Mr. Datay was out of town on February 23, 2014.
>
> Question: Where was Mr. Datay on February 23, 2014?
>
> Answer: He was in Cleveland all day on February 23, 2014.
>
> Question: How do you know that Mr. Datay was in Cleveland on February 23, 2014?
>
> Answer: I make his travel arrangements. I remember buying his ticket for that trip to Cleveland. He left at 6:30 a.m. from Santa Anna and did not get back until almost midnight that day. And I was in the office on February 23, 2014 and I know that Mr. Datay was not in the office in Anaheim that day.
>
> Question: Did you see Mr. Datay get on the plane to Cincinnati on February 23, 2014?
>
> Answer: No.
>
> Question: Did you communicate with Mr. Datay in any way on February 23, 2014?
>
> Answer: I don't remember.
>
> Question: How do you know Mr. Datay actually traveled to Cleveland on February 23, 2014?
>
> Answer: I guess I don't know for sure.

5.3.2   LISTENING FOR AND EXPLORING UNEXPECTED INFORMATION

Almost every deposition will reveal some information or issue that the attorney will find unexpected, making it difficult to strictly follow an initial interview outline with a list of topics. In fact, it is important not to just plow through an outline when the deponent raises entirely new topics of importance that that attorney hadn't considered beforehand, has a wholly unexpected attitude or affect, adds unanticipated facts, or even

---

[8]For a succinct guide to dealing with hostile witnesses and hostile opposing counsel, see BRADLEY G. CLARY ET AL., SUCCESSFUL FIRST DEPOSITIONS 127–61 (3rd ed. 2011).

just displays a revealing gesture that needs to be probed.   Nothing identifies a rookie deposing attorney more quickly than observing the attorney plow through a deposition outline and ignore the deponent's answers not directly responsive to questions.

The challenge for the deposing attorney is to listen carefully for this type of unexpected information and incorporate it into the questioning while maintaining an organized approach to the deposition. The attorney has to make a quick decision whether to follow-up the unexpected information immediately and thus drop the current topic, or delay the inquiry until later in the interview. Again, there is no "correct" way to proceed. It depends on context. Yet it is important to consider your options for handling the situation and to prepare for the need to be flexible in your approach to the interview outline.

Let's turn again to the gas exposure case presented in Section 2.1 as an example. Consider that in the midst of deposing Ms. McDonald, she states, "I met with Dr. Tangier on the 16th. I am sure about that because the 16th was the day for visiting my parole officer that month." One response by the attorney for Bi-Tell might be to ask, "What kind of felon are you?!" That probably would be the wrong response. A better approach would be to nod and just make a note to follow-up later in the interview about this matter. But it might be equally effective to acknowledge that this is important information and ask McDonald something like, "Tell me about your parole visits?," thereby inviting a discussion of the underlying criminal history. In other words, start a new topic with an open-ended question. The important point is that the attorney listens carefully to the deponent and incorporates the new information into the examination.

It may be helpful to remember that you can pause and slow down. Unless your deposition is being videotaped to be played at trial because the witness will be unavailable to testify, you will only be using excerpts from the deposition at trial or in your motion briefing. The judge or jury will never know that you paused for a bit before asking a question.[9]

---

[9] Slowing down when needed in a deposition also can help with "tics," which is a common problem experienced in an attorney's first few depositions.   Everything said in a deposition will be transcribed as long as you are "on record;" in other words, until the attorney who noticed the deposition asks the court reporter to stop transcribing the discussion. Many attorneys engaging in their first formal questioning develop some form of tic. A common example of this behavior is to begin almost every question by saying "OK," "alright" or the like.   Sometimes the tic is repeating the last few words of the witness or any of a variety of other behaviors. The completed recorded can end up looking like this:

Question: OK. Why did you call Mr. Bronson on February 15?

Answer: He asked me to call him.

Question: OK. What time of day did you make that call to Mr. Bronson on February 15?

Answer: About 2:00. Not earlier than that.

Question: OK, 2:00. You mean 2:00 p.m., in the afternoon?

Answer: Yes.

5.4 PRACTICAL MATTERS

This chapter briefly describes basic deposition procedures and practice. The deposition simulation introduces questioning to build a formal record for students who may not have completed a course in evidence or trial practice. This chapter summarizes the use of objections by opposing counsel in depositions and handling documents during the examination.

5.4.1   OPENING AND CLOSING THE DEPOSITION

Depositions have a ritual starting procedure. A court reporter almost always will be present at the deposition and will record the examination. The court reporter will begin the deposition by identifying all the people at the deposition and by swearing in the witness. After the deponent is sworn in, the attorney can start questioning.

Several lines of introductory directions and questions are commonly employed at the start of a deposition. Some attorneys ask all of these types of questions, while others will employ just one or two of these introductory inquiries. Introductory remarks and questions include the following:

Introductions. The attorney states the case name, whom she represents and perhaps briefly explains the nature of the suit.

Proper response directions (questions). The attorney explains to the deponent the need to answer in a manner that allows for the effective creation of a written record. These requirements include the use of verbal response rather than gestures, that the deponent must let the attorney finish asking questions and that the witness and attorney should not talk over each other, and that the deponent should ask the attorney to explain or re-ask any question that the deponent does not understand. The attorney then will have the deponent acknowledge understanding of these requirements. For example:

> Question: Do you understand that a court reporter will be recording our conversation?
>
> Answer: Yes.
>
> Question: That means that you need to respond verbally and not just with a gesture. Do you understand that?
>
> Answer: Yes.

Attorneys want the deponent to understand the necessity to interact in a formal, recorded examination, but the attorneys also can have other

---

Question: OK. Why do you know it was not earlier than 2:00 p.m. on February 15 that you called Mr. Bronson?

Think about having to read at trial this transcript with all the "OK" beginnings. Periodically reflecting for a few seconds before asking a question may help you avoid this fate.

objectives in asking such questions. These questions make it clear to the deponent that the attorney is in control of the deposition, which improves the attorney's chance of getting the deponent to respond to questions and avoid disruptive conduct with hostile witnesses. Second, the attorney can use this record later in the deposition or at trial to establish that the deponent had agreed to rules for the examination, such as that the deponent will ask the attorney if he does not understand a question.

Proper response directions (objections). The attorney explains that objections by another attorney at the deposition (other than an instruction not to answer when asserting a privilege) should not stop the deponent from answering the question.

Deponent's capacity. The attorney inquires about the deponent's health, physical and mental, at the time of the deposition. This inquiry provides some protection against the deponent later claiming that she was ill or disoriented at the time a deposition answer was provided. Some attorneys will routinely inquire about whether the deponent has taken medications, drank alcohol or ingested other substances that could negatively affect the deponent's cognition. These questions might also result in the deponent recoiling from the attorney before the substantive examination begins, so weigh carefully whether this type of questioning is worth it.

Breaks. The attorney explains that she will stop the depositions at predetermined times to allow the deponent a break from the proceeding, and then obtain the deponent's agreement to this procedure. Attorneys use this agreement to prevent (or attempt to prevent) the deponent from requesting a break for the purpose of delaying a response to a difficult question.

Prior deposition experience. Most attorneys inquire at the outset about whether the deponent has been deposed before, and then use that information to couch the remaining introductory remarks and inquiries (e.g., "As you know, in a deposition you cannot use gestures..."). Asking the deponent about prior deposition experience can provide useful information about the deponent's experiences. Follow-up with detailed questions about prior deposition experience if the deponent states she has been deposed previously.

At the close of a deposition, attorneys usually will inform the deponent of his right to review and correct the deposition transcript within 30 days after notice that the transcript is completed.[10] The attorney usually will ask the deponent if he wants to waive this right. If the deponent refuses to waive the right of review, the attorney will discuss arrangements with the deponent, or his attorney if represented, and the court reporter about making available a copy of the transcript for review.

---

[10] FED. R. CIV. P. 30(e).

5.4.2   MAKING AND HANDLING OBJECTIONS IN A DEPOSITION

Deposition questions, like witness examination at trial, can incur an objection by an opposing attorney. The opposing attorney may be representing the deponent or may be representing an opposing party, or both. Below is a brief description of some of the most common objections voiced during a deposition.

1. *Ambiguous*: The question is unclear or subject to multiple interpretations as to the information sought from the witness. Example: "How large is your company?"

2. *Compound question*: The question contains two independent inquiries. Example: "Did the car run the red light going over 40 miles per hour?"

3. *Calls for speculation*: Asks the witness to provide information not in his or her personal knowledge. Example: "What was Smith thinking when you said that Jones was incompetent?"

4. *Argumentative*: Argues with what the witness has stated. Example: "You can't possibly mean what you just said about the value of the house?"

5. *Asked and answered*: Asks a question that was previously asked by the deposing attorney and answered by the witness. Example: "Question: Were you on the street or the sidewalk? Answer: Neither. I was on the strip of grass between the sidewalk and curb. Question: So you were on the sidewalk?"

Objections as to the form of the question do not stop the deponent from answering the question because no judge is present to rule on the objection.[11] You are making the objection for the record. The deposing attorney has the option of re-phrasing the question if he or she determines your objection is valid, or to ignore it. Objections are made without argumentation and succinctly. Failure to make an objection as to the form of the question results in waiver of the right to that objection if the deposition testimony is read at trial.[12]

The opposing counsel should make an objection as to the form of the question when it is proper <u>and</u> strategic. In other words, it is not in the interest of the opposing attorney to voice every valid objection. When the objection allows the deposing attorney the opportunity to reflect on a question and re-phrase to a more specific and accurate inquiry, the objection can actually benefit the deposing attorney.

---

[11] Attorneys can instruct their client (but not an unrepresented person) not to answer a question if that question seeks privileged information, such as disclosure of an attorney-client conversation or information that has been deemed confidential.

[12] FED. R. CIV. P. 32(d)(3).

5.4.3   MECHANICS OF USING DOCUMENTS IN A DEPOSITION

Attorneys often ask the deponent questions about documents during a deposition. Documents used during the deposition are marked by number and appended to the transcript of the deposition.

The deposing attorney or the court reporter can handle the marking of exhibits in any manner that accomplishes the goal of uniquely identifying each document used during the deposition. Attorneys often will sequentially mark documents, or ask the court reporter to mark documents, as the documents are used during the deposition. Some attorneys will occasionally or habitually pre-mark all documents that might be used in each deposition they conduct. It doesn't matter how the documents get a number, just make sure they are uniquely identifiable.

The usual process in a deposition is for the attorney to show the marked document to the witness and inquire whether the deponent recognizes the document.[13] A typical exchange could appear as follows:

> Question: I am showing you a document marked Exhibit 5. Do you recognize this document?
>
> Answer: Yes. That's an email I wrote to Felicia Turner.
>
> Question: Did you send this email to Ms. Turner on the date indicated on the document, which is November 3, 2013?
>
> Answer: Yes.

The attorney then inquires about the document. The specific inquiry will be shaped by the attorney's purpose in employing the document in the deposition.

---

[13] This inquiry is part of an evidentiary requirement to establish "foundation" of a document for purposes of establishing the admissibility of the document into evidence. A full explanation of establishing the requirements for admission of documents will occur in study of evidence and trial procedure.

CHAPTER 6

PROFESSIONAL RESPONSIBILITY IN PRACTICE

■ ■ ■

This chapter outlines foundational professional responsibility concepts. Understanding these concepts helps attorneys identify ethical issues that arise on an almost daily basis in the practice of law. These are not dramatic dilemmas like a gun in the client's duffle bag or cocaine coated money presented to the attorney as a retainer. Instead, these are concerns that arise routinely in practice. Compliance with the rules that govern the attorney's relationship with the client is an everyday concern in the practice of law. The bulk of these professional and ethical issues require good business practices, a balanced view of one's own abilities, professional and personal organization, and knowledge of the law of professional responsibility.

Section 6.1 offers an overview of the numerous laws governing attorney conduct. Section 6.2 is a brief introduction to the ethical rules governing the legal profession. In Section 4.3.1, we introduced a portion of the Model Rules of Professional Conduct relating to communications with non-clients. Section 6.3 focuses on the part of the Model Rules of Professional Conduct that establish the attorney's duties to clients.

6.1 THE LAW OF LAWYERING

The Model Rules of Professional Conduct are just one part of a vast body of law that can result in consequences resulting from the actions of the attorney. Detailed below is some of the law governing the conduct of attorneys.

Malpractice Liability. Attorneys, like other professionals, can be liable to their clients for malpractice. Most attorneys secure malpractice insurance. When the attorney applies for such insurance, the insurer as part of the underwriting process will ask the attorney or law firm questions about data management and storage, practice areas, conflict of interest tracking, and calendar systems (to insure the attorney does not miss important deadlines or court dates). If the attorney or law firm cannot adequately represent that the law practice is organized according to the potential insurer's expectations, coverage will not be extended.

In 2004, the American Bar Association (ABA) approved the Model Court Rule on Insurance Disclosure, which calls for states to require any attorney engaged in private practice to annually certify to the highest court of that state whether she is currently covered by professional liability insurance, and to notify the court if the insurance policy lapses or terminates.[1] The ABA recommends that the state's highest court make this information available to the public.

Agency Law. As defined by the Restatement (Second) of Agency, "[a]gency is the fiduciary relation which results from the manifestation of consent by one person to another that the other shall act on his behalf and subject to his control, and consent by the other so to act."[2] Attorneys are agents of their clients. This principal/agent relationship is most obvious when an attorney is, for example, representing a client in negotiation or in tendering an offer of settlement in a letter. The fact that the attorney must obtain the client's authority to negotiate or tender offers, and cannot accept an offer without the authority of the client, necessarily affects attorney behavior. Attorneys who do not comply with the requirements imposed on an agent are subject to liability for breach of fiduciary duty.

Rules of Civil Procedure or Other Court Rules. The rules of civil procedure—whether state or federal—set forth a host of requirements bearing on an attorney's behavior in litigation. Some of these rules provide for sanctions on attorneys that violate the rules, including asserting frivolous or unsupported claims in pleadings and other written submissions to the court,[3] improperly using the civil subpoena process,[4] or failing to abide by limits on and requirements for the use of discovery.[5] Other rules of court instruct an attorney as to proper behavior. The requirements of court rules range from appropriate dress to time limits on performing certain acts. The rules of court, like the rules of civil procedure, often vary by particular area of law, such as the special rules that can exist for juvenile, probate, adoption, criminal, family and tax matters.

Trial Court's Inherent Power. The trial court possesses the inherent power to sanction attorneys for failing to comply with the court's directives, including sanctions for contempt when the attorney fails to abide by instructions issued by a judge or flagrantly defies ethical and

---

[1] MODEL COURT RULE ON INSURANCE DISCLOSURE (2004).

[2] RESTATEMENT (SECOND) OF AGENCY § 1 (1958). There are some actions an attorney undertakes (as officer of the court, for example) where the attorney is not acting as an agent of the client. Deborah A. DeMott, *The Lawyer as Agent*, 67 FORDHAM L. REV. 301, 301 (1998).

[3] FED. R. CIV. P. 11. State statutes sometimes replicate the obligations imposed on attorneys in rules of civil procedure providing for sanctions in cases where attorneys assert frivolous claims or propound discovery for improper purposes. *See, e.g.*, MINN. STAT. § 549.211 (1997).

[4] FED. R. CIV. P. 45.

[5] FED. R. CIV. P. 37.

proper standards of behavior.[6] Attorneys are not entitled to any more notice than knowledge of basic standards of conduct or a trial court's clear instruction. Contempt can include a range of sanctions, including fines and jail time, and is a sharp tool to encourage proper behavior by attorneys.[7]

Criminal Law. Although not common, attorneys may be prosecuted for crimes committed in the course of representing a client. The case of New York attorney Lynne Stewart highlights the exposure of an attorney to criminal liability in her role as agent of the client. After a seven-month trial, Ms. Stewart was convicted on charges of conspiracy to aid and abet terrorism, defrauding the U.S. government, and violating a government Bureau of Prisons Special Administrative Order when she released a press statement from her imprisoned client, the Egyptian cleric Omar Abdel Rachman.[8]

The remainder of this chapter addresses one particularly important area of law of special concern to attorneys—the ethical rules embodied in the Model Rules of Professional Conduct.

6.2 INTRODUCTION TO ATTORNEY ETHICAL REQUIREMENTS

An attorney must obtain a license from a state entity before she can practice law. The licensing agency, whether a bar association or the highest court in a particular jurisdiction, establishes rules or delegates rule-making authority so the attorneys in that jurisdiction have a clear understanding of how to behave in order to maintain their licenses. The state entity in charge of attorney licensing and discipline is named differently in various states. For example, Massachusetts attorneys are licensed by the Board of Bar Overseers while Illinois attorneys are licensed by the Attorney Registration & Disciplinary Commission. Each state also adopts and interprets its own ethical rules, but most states have adopted in whole or in part the Model Rules of Professional Conduct promulgated by the American Bar Association.

The rules of professional conduct are not aspirational; they set forth mandatory and minimum standards of conduct. The comments to the rules provide explanations and guidance in specific circumstances. The American Bar Association and state authorities also issue opinions to

---

[6] Adriana M. Chavez, *El Paso Attorney Stuart Leeds Requests Reduced Jail Sentence on Contempt Charge,* EL PASO TIMES, June 25, 2013,,indicating the judge found Leeds made "false and material misrepresentations" to the court in a criminal case against Leeds' client.

[7] Contempt is rarely used. In *Legal Ethics: Law Stories*, Deborah Rhode and David Luban refer to the reluctance of judges to criticize the conduct of attorneys and a general unwillingness on the part of the bench to discuss and enforce ethics rules because "... most judges are former trial lawyers and identify with the difficulties of the role." Rhode and Luban characterize this unwillingness as "a continuing and important form of professional failure." *Id.* at 183 n.9.

[8] United States v. Stewart, 590 F.3d 93 (2d Cir. 2009).

provide attorneys guidance on particular situations. For example, the intersection of ethics and technology has prompted several guidance opinions. One such issue is when storage of private client data using cloud computing is permissible.[9] A related topic concerns metadata or confidential client information embedded in electronic documents. Metadata may consist of identifiers and revisions to documents that cling to the document and may be discovered by an adverse party when the document is viewed in an electronic format.[10]

In some jurisdictions, an attorney with an ethical question can obtain a confidential advisory opinion on how to manage the situation.[11] In addition, law firms sometimes have committees to handle ethical questions and review firm policies to ensure rule compliance. Law firms and attorneys dedicate substantial resources to rule compliance as an investment in the firm's assets, including its reputation.

6.3 THE FIVE C'S—PROFESSIONAL RESPONSIBILITIES TO CLIENTS

The attorney and client relationship can be one of the most frustrating aspects of practicing law, but if managed well it can also be one of the most satisfying. The satisfaction can come in a variety of forms—from helping a client in distress, to assisting a client organize her personal affairs, to representing a client organizing a new corporate venture. The frustration also can come in a variety of forms—from listening to a client weep after receiving an adverse decision, to delivering the news that a client's business is being investigated, to learning of a client's failure to abide by a court order. When the attorney-client relationship is not managed properly, it can be consequential, as well as frustrating. Unhappy clients sometimes will not pay an account and rarely will be a

---

[9] Bar organizations in at least a dozen jurisdictions have issued advisory opinions on cloud computing services. In Nevada, for example, the State Bar of Nevada's Standing Committee on Ethics and Professional Responsibility issued Opinion 33 on February 9, 2006, which indicated that storing client information on a cloud computing service did not amount to a breach of client confidences. Opinion 33 went on to direct that a Nevada attorney should use reasonable care in selection and use of cloud computing services and specifically should chose a vendor that can be reasonably relied on to maintain the confidentiality of client information.

[10] The advisory opinions handle this topic differently depending on the jurisdiction and generally turn on how a jurisdiction handles inadvertent disclosure of confidential information to a third party. In addition to the state organizations that have issued opinions on metadata, the American Bar Association Standing Committee on Ethics and Professional Responsibility issued Formal Opinion 06–442 (detailing safeguards such as document "scrubbing" to remove metadata) and Formal Opinion 05–437 (directing that an attorney receiving metadata he knows or should know has been inadvertently disclosed to notify the sender). Related advisory opinions address website content, HIPPA and the disclosure of a client's medical data in litigation.

[11] Some of the jurisdictions offering this type of "hotline" assistance for attorneys include Alaska, Arizona, California, Colorado, Florida, Indiana, Kentucky, Louisiana, Maryland, Michigan, Minnesota, New Jersey, New Mexico, Pennsylvania, South Carolina, and Virginia, and several municipal bar organizations such as Cincinnati, Cleveland, and Columbus, Ohio, and New York, New York.

source of future referrals. Unhappy clients can also be the cause of complaints to the licensing authority.

The ethical rules governing the attorney-client relationship are shaped by what some commentators have referred to as "the 5 Cs"—competence, control, communication, confidentiality, and conflicts of interest. [12] Each of these duties is described in the subsections below.

6.3.1   COMPETENCE

Model Rule 1.1 sets forth the duty of the attorney to possess adequate legal knowledge and expertise to handle the matter presented by the client. This Rule requires the attorney to be competent in matters before he or she agrees to represent a client. One of the primary reasons attorneys practice in firms is the collective judgment and knowledge that increases the competence of all the attorneys in the firm. The practice of law is fraught with uncertainty, and practicing within a firm (with attorneys who communicate with each other, discuss their cases, and benefit from each other's knowledge and experience) provides the attorney with more resources to avoid incompetence.

> *Example:* Attorney Smith is retained by an entrepreneur, Carl West, to negotiate a commercial lease for his nail salon. Smith interviews West on several occasions and learns about the proposed nail salon, the specific ventilation needs of the nail salon Mr. West hopes to build, and exterior modifications Mr. West wants to make to the existing commercial space. During one such interview, Mr. West asks the following question, "You know, I created a ton of graphic nail designs at the salon where I was working last year. The owner of that salon said he owned them because I created them on his time, and several were posted to his salon's website. Can you tell me who owns those designs?"
>
> Attorney Smith has no experience or training in intellectual property matters, nor has Smith been retained to assist the client with this type of matter. Each attorney needs to assess their own circumstances and, depending on the size of the firm and the attorney's contacts, respond to the client. If the attorney does not have expertise in intellectual property issues, one proper response is to refer the client to another attorney more equipped to handle that particular issue. If handled appropriately (i.e., referring the client to a reliable attorney with the requisite expertise), a referral will add value both to the client and to the attorney's network of business contacts.

---

[12] *See e.g.,* LAWRENCE J. FOX & SUSAN R. MARTYN, RED FLAGS: A LAWYER'S HANDBOOK ON LEGAL ETHICS 65 (2005).

6.3.2   CLIENT CONTROL

Model Rule 1.2 concerns the allocation of authority between the attorney and the client. The Rule places the objectives of the representation in the hands of the client, and requires an attorney to consult with the client on the means by which to pursue the client's objectives. The Rule expressly states that the client decides whether to accept or reject a settlement offer.

In practice, many decisions fall within a gray area where the attorney suggests a means to accomplish the client's objectives, but it is up the client decides whether the "means" (for example, a motion for summary judgment) is worth it. The client may pay for the motion costs, depending on the fee arrangement, and definitely will suffer the consequences of success or failure of the motion. One group of scholars has proposed the following "substantial impact standard" to assist the attorney in making this determination: "Lawyers should provide clients with the opportunity to make decisions whenever a reasonably prudent and diligent lawyer would or should know that a pending decision is likely to have a substantial legal or non-legal impact on clients."[13]   Even in situations where the attorney gets to make the final decision, the decision needs to be explained to the client so that the client understands and takes responsibility for the decision.

> *Example:* Consider a litigation matter between two businesses. The plaintiff company wants not only compensation, but payback. The plaintiff asks her attorney to subpoena and depose the former assistant to a vice president at the defendant company. The plaintiff makes this request not because it knows this particular assistant has vital information or evidence. Instead, the plaintiff tells the attorney that the former assistant is a relative of the vice president of defendant and the purpose of the request is to annoy the defendant's management and create additional pressure on the company to settle the case .

> Using subpoena power in the manner requested by the client is inappropriate, and contrary to the rules of civil procedure and ethical rules. The attorney, therefore, must decide this issue because the attorney's law license is threatened if she misuses the subpoena power. The client does not call the shots when it comes to actions that could impair the attorney's license.

6.3.3   COMMUNICATION

Model Rule 1.4 covers the attorney's duty to adequately and appropriately communicate with clients. Clients must be kept reasonably informed of

---

[13] DAVID A. BINDER, ET AL., LAWYERS AS COUNSELORS: A CLIENT CENTERED APPROACH 277 (2d ed. 1991).

the status of the case and provided with enough information to make decisions. A failure to communicate is at the root of most ethical complaints against lawyers.[14] One frequent cause of attorneys' failures to communicate is avoidance of telling the client bad news, especially when the client is already upset about a matter. It can also be difficult to report a mixed outcome where the next strategic step is unclear.

> *Example*: Attorney Jasper is representing Ari Ali, a client in a marriage dissolution proceeding. Jasper attends a telephonic review hearing. The individuals participating in the call include Jasper, the attorney representing Ali's wife, and the judge. During the telephone call, the call participants discuss the progress of the case, and specifically address the informal exchange of documents and possible mediation regarding the division of assets and custody. When the call ends, Jasper immediately contacts Mr. Ali and describes the content of the telephone call. They collaborate on a strategy to gather the necessary documents. Jasper also inquires as to Mr. Ali's preferences regarding mediation, including cost and timing.

By immediately contacting the client, attorney Jasper not only executes the duty to communicate with the client, but Jasper is engaging the client in the necessary work of marshalling facts and making choices about the direction of the litigation. Prompt and thorough client engagement is essential. Finally, and this is no small point, Mr. Ali may be more likely to promptly pay the attorney's bill knowing that he was included in the details of what occurred, and participated in the direction of the case by talking to his attorney immediately thereafter.

6.3.4 CONFIDENTIALITY

Rule 1.6 establishes the duty to keep all information related to the representation of a client confidential. Rule 1.6 means that a lawyer never discusses client matters with anyone outside the law firm. This includes all information acquired from or transmitted to the client. The duty to retain the client's confidences supersedes the satisfaction of describing one's cases and work. Managing inquiries from colleagues and friends regarding legal work falls squarely on the attorney.[15] Section 14.1.2 explores how to explain confidentiality to prospective or new clients.

---

[14] Stephen E. Schemenauer, *What We've Got Here . . . Is a Failure . . . to Communicate: A Statistical Analysis of the Nation's Most Common Ethical Complaints*, 30 HAMLINE L. REV. 629, 631 (2007).

[15] The duty of confidentiality is related to, but broader than, the concept of attorney/client privilege which is a rule of evidence.

Example: Revisit the example in 6.3.1 above. Attorney Smith's fact investigation in preparation for negotiation of West's commercial lease is nearly complete and Smith has compiled a thick file on the matter. Smith has a copy of every piece of written correspondence exchanged on the matter (including his retainer with West and numerous emails), as well as sample provisions for the commercial lease, architectural drawings, and copies of West's business organization documents. Smith has decided that a site visit is essential to get a feel for the proposed location of West's Ethiopian restaurant. Smith wants to take photographs, inspect the parking area, and assess the variety and quality of businesses in the surrounding area. Smith takes the West file from his law office, and drives to the proposed site.

During and after the site visit, Smith makes several deliberate decisions to execute his duty of confidentiality to West. First, Smith moves the West file from the passenger area of his vehicle to the trunk where it will be safe. Smith also does this because the label on the file clearly states "J. West – Commercial Lease Negotiation," And someone passing by the car may see this label. Second, while Smith is at the site, he decides to call West and describe for West his immediate impressions. Smith makes the phone call from inside his vehicle, instead of from the sidewalk café near the proposed site. A call from inside the car is the only way for Smith to protect the confidentiality of his conversation with West. Third, Smith drives directly home after the site visit, instead of returning to the office. Smith removes the West file from his vehicle and brings it into his apartment. The parking lot is insecure—it is not well lit and several vehicles have been broken into during the previous year. Smith's deliberate choices are examples of how an attorney might manage his obligations and duty of confidentiality to the client.

6.3.5   CONFLICTS OF INTEREST

Rules 1.7 through 1.10 regulate conflicts of interest, which is generally defined as an interest of the attorney arising from the representation of a client that may conflict with duties owed to another client. An attorney must be entirely dedicated to her clients and a conflict of interest can undermine that dedication. The rules on conflict of interest are designed, in part, to protect the independent judgment at the core of an attorney's responsibilities to the client.

The conflict of interest rules apply to relationships with both current and former clients, although the exact contour of those duties varies between current and former clients. After the active attorney client relationship has ended, the attorney must uphold duties of loyalty and confidentiality to former clients.[16] A conflict of interest as to one attorney applies to any attorney with whom that attorney practices in a law firm.[17]

The existence of a conflict does not always mean that the attorney cannot represent a prospective client. Some conflicts can be waived by written consent of the attorney's current or former client and the written consent of the prospective client.[18]

One important implication of the conflicts of interest rules is that attorneys must determine prior to accepting a new client whether representing that client will cause a conflict of interest with the attorney's duties to her other current and former clients. In executing her duty to determine whether a conflict of interest exists, the attorney must have in place procedures appropriate for the size and type of practice to determine the persons and issues involved. This process is commonly referred to as "a conflicts check." If the attorney fails to exercise due diligence in a conflicts check, the comments to the Rules specifically instruct that ignorance of a conflict "caused by a failure to institute such procedures will not excuse a lawyer's violation of this Rule."[19] Because of the rule imputing an interest of each attorney in the firm to other attorneys in the firm, conflicts checks in large law firms can be especially difficult to ascertain and manage. [20]

> *Example*: An attorney is considering LKN Enterprises, Inc., as a prospective client. The potential adverse party is Barrel BonBons, Ltd. The dispute regards a shipment of chocolate by Barrel BonBons to LKN that LKN believes was tainted. Barrel BonBons refused to cure the defect and LKN sustained damages for its failure to honor several contracts with its suppliers.
>
> Before the attorney interviews an official from LKN about the dispute, the attorney entered the following entities into her law firm's conflicts check system: LKN Enterprises, Inc. (potential client) and Barrel BonBons, Ltd. (adverse party).
>
> The conflicts check reveals that the attorney was retained by a group of three women to conduct a pre-litigation investigation of

---

[16] MODEL RULES OF PROF'L CONDUCT R. 1.9 (2012).

[17] MODEL RULES OF PROF'L CONDUCT R. 1.10 (2012).

[18] MODEL RULES OF PROF'L CONDUCT R. 1.7(b) (2012).

[19] MODEL RULES OF PROF'L CONDUCT R. 1.7 cmt. 3 (2012).

[20] The recent case of Covington and Burling, LLP, City of Lake Elmo, Metropolitan Council vs. 3M Corp., No. A12–1867, 2013 Westlaw 3284285 (Minn. Ct. App. July 1, 2013), showcases the disastrous effects—for both attorneys and clients—of ignoring the rules regarding conflicts. The Minnesota Court of Appeals upheld the trial court's disqualification of plaintiffs' counsel, the D.C.-based law firm of Covington and Burling, in response to defendant 3M's motion to disqualify the law firm. Defendant 3M was a former client of Covington and Burling. The court found Covington and Burling's former representation of 3M "substantially related" to the litigation Covington and Burling was pursing against 3M on behalf of plaintiffs. The law firm had spent three years representing the plaintiffs when it was disqualified.

a potential employment discrimination suit against LKN. The attorney maintained a file on the matter, but the case never developed into a lawsuit because, shortly after the attorney was retained, each of the clients had been promoted (albeit more slowly than their male counterparts) by LKN.

The attorney has to determine if this situation presents a conflict that will prevent her from representing LKN. Using the language of Rule 1.7(a)(2), the attorney determines whether her ability to represent LKN Enterprises, Inc., is materially limited in any way by her duties to the former clients. Material limitation, if it exists, should be disclosed to and discussed with the client and the client should have the opportunity to consent to it (i.e., waive the conflict of interest)[21] or find legal representation elsewhere.[22] Material limitation can arise from the constellation of contacts that the attorney or the potential client or adverse party has with any other person.

Here, there likely is no material limitation. As former clients of the attorney, the three women are entitled to confidentiality and loyalty.[23] The attorney can uphold those duties without it affecting LKN in its potential lawsuit against Barrel BonBons. The attorney will maintain the confidentiality of the file by not disclosing any detail of the representation to LKN.

---

[21] Asking a client to waive a conflict of interest based on a material limitation is not a seamless process. The attorney first needs to determine whether she can disclose sufficient information to the potential client, while upholding duties to other current or former clients, for example, so the potential client can make a knowing waiver. If it is not possible for the potential client to make a knowing waiver, the attorney simply cannot represent the potential client.

[22] Rule 1.7 sets the basic rules of conflicts and is the foundation around which attorneys create databases and other tools to identify conflicts. Rule 1.8 concerns special issues with current clients and concerns mainly overreaching by the attorney. The comments to Rule 1.8 illustrate and advise against any dynamic where an attorney, who has superior knowledge and may be coordinating a situation, improperly benefits at the expense of the client.

[23] MODEL RULES OF PROF'L CONDUCT R. 1.9 (2012).

CHAPTER 7

INTRODUCTION TO ADVOCACY

■ ■ ■

Attorneys are zealous advocates on behalf of their clients before judges, juries, and in non-judicial forums. Attorneys are counselors who listen to the client's goals and confidentially advise the client about how to proceed in a matter. Attorneys are negotiators who bargain with opposing counsel to resolve disputes or structure transactions. All of these skills are in addition to legal analysis (knowing legal doctrine, research and analysis), fact-gathering (effective interviewing and related tasks), and the capacity to manage the fact-law iterative dynamic.

Chapters 7 through 11 introduce advocacy, negotiation and counseling skills, with a focus on use of these skills as practiced by attorneys in dispute resolution. This chapter examines some basic concepts underlying effective advocacy. Chapter 8 introduces distributive negotiating theory, an approach to negotiations that often describes litigation settlement efforts. Advocacy and negotiation skills are critical to almost any practicing attorney. The next three chapters relate these skills to simulations you will be completing. Chapter 9 discusses negotiating and advocacy in the context of drafting or responding to a written settlement offer letter. Chapter 10 looks at appearances by attorneys before a judge in chambers. Chapter 11 introduces some basic principles of client counseling and discusses effective participation in mediation.

The attorney as advocate conjures an image of a closing argument at trial, or the like. Advocacy is much more than public presentation skills. Business law attorneys, for example, are advocates for their clients and often engage in persuading other parties to shape favorable transaction terms. This chapter looks at three aspects of advocacy by attorneys: finding and using narrative (Section 7.1), identifying and understanding the target of persuasion (Section 7.2), and awareness of the policy implications and context of advocacy (Section 7.3).

7.1 PERSUASION THROUGH NARRATIVE

Think about one of the cases you read recently for a law school class. How would you describe the case and its holding if you were asked by the course instructor to present the case to the class? Now think about how you would describe the case to your aunt or uncle (assuming that these relatives are not attorneys). Your description to a non-attorney presumably would be more of a narrative—an explanation of the events in the form of a story.

Cases almost always are constructed by the attorney rather than presented at the outset as a coherent whole. It is the attorney's responsibility to work on two inter-related levels in creating the case. Part of the attorney's work is the painstaking job of identifying or gathering key facts to support or disprove each element of a possible legal claim or defense. The cliché, "thinking like a lawyer," is typically used to refer to this process of deconstructing facts into legal elements. Practicing attorneys know that creating compelling narratives is equally important to the attorney's work, and narrative creation works from a different set of premises.

7.1.1   THE IMPORTANCE OF NARRATIVE

Narrative is critical to effective advocacy because it is how people grasp the essence of the problems presented by human conflict and ventures. Law Professor Anthony Amsterdam and Psychology Professor Jerome Bruner describe narrative as the means by which attorneys "make it humanly possible" to relate the fundamental value judgments underlying the law "to the current particularities of the cases we adjudicate or arbitrate or negotiate, or those in which we help our clients comprehend the circumstances of their lives within the framework of the law or vice versa."[1] Professors Amsterdam and Bruner recount an anecdote from Justice Hugo Black, a native of Alabama, about the power of narrative to shape decision-making.

> A jury in rural Alabama was called to try a poor farmer charged with stealing a mule from a rich one. The jury's first verdict was: "Not guilty, provided he returns the mule." The judge refused to accept the verdict, telling the jury that it was impermissibly conditional. The jury resumed deliberations and rendered a second verdict: "Not guilty, but he has to return the mule." When the judge again rejected the verdict, telling the jury that it was impermissibly contradictory, the jury came back with a third verdict, which the judge finally accepted: "Not guilty, let him keep the damn mule."[2]

It is easy to imagine how narrative is used in the legal profession when you think about a criminal prosecutor telling a jury the story of a violent assault, or a Depression-era criminal defense attorney representing a poor farmer who stole a mule. The use of narrative, however, is central to the work of attorneys even in more technical fields. The importance of

---

[1] ANTHONY G. AMSTERDAM & JEROME BRUNER, MINDING THE LAW 141 (2000) (emphasis omitted).

[2] *Id.* at 118.

narrative in legal advocacy has been described in a variety of legal disciplines.[3]

Consider a well-known antitrust suit against Microsoft Corporation by the United States Department of Justice. Professor Joshua Newberg has dissected the trial in that case to identify the narratives of the two parties. He identifies the government's narrative as follows:

> [Microsoft responded to a competitive threat in the browser market] by bundling the Internet Explorer browser with the Windows operating system, excluding Netscape's Navigator browser from major distribution channels through licensing incentives and restrictions, and drawing users toward Microsoft's Windows-only version of JAVA and away from Sun's cross-platform version. As a result of Microsoft's campaign against the "middleware threat," nascent platform competition from Netscape and Sun was crushed, innovation—particularly on the part of OEMs—was suppressed, and consumers endured both higher prices and inferior personal computer software and complementary products."[4]

Microsoft's opposing narrative switched the vantage point from a battle between competitors to a battle between Microsoft and a government agency seeking "extraordinary intervention in the marketplace." Microsoft argued that the Department of Justice had brought a case designed to "shield huge companies like AOL, Netscape, IBM, and Sun from the rigors of competition."[5]

7.1.2   CONSTRUCTING NARRATIVE

Creating a narrative is different than presenting factual disputes or legal arguments. Litigants typically will have very different narratives even when the facts are undisputed. The attorney constructs the narrative by highlighting and sequencing facts in a way that evokes sympathy for the concerns or position of the client, or focuses blame on another person.[6]

Attorneys will sometimes emphasize facts that are not strongly probative, or even especially relevant, to the elements of proof for the claims or

---

[3] *See, e.g.,* Allan Kanner & Tibor L. Nagy, *Legal Strategy, Storytelling and Complex Litigation,* 30 AM. J. TRIAL ADVOC. 1, 13 (2006) (toxic tort cases); Roberta Rosenthal Kwall, *Narrative's Implications for Moral Rights and Copyright's Joint Authorship Doctrine,* 75 S. CAL. L. REV. 1 (2001) (copyright law); Pamela A. Wilkins, *Confronting the Invisible Witness: The Use of Narrative to Neutralize Capital Jurors' Implicit Racial Biases,* 115 W. VA. L. REV. 305 (2012) (criminal law).

[4] Joshua A. Newberg, *The Narrative Construction of Antitrust,* 12 S. CAL. INTERDISC. L. J. 181 (2003).

[5] *Id.* at 192.

[6] Professors Amsterdam and Bruner explicate in detail the role and structure of narrative in the legal profession. They describe the "bare-bones" building blocks of narrative in a five part sequence that includes a "steady state" disrupted by a "trouble" and ultimately "restored" (or "transformed") by the events at issue. Amsterdam & Bruner, *supra* note 1, at 113–14.

defenses at issue because those facts tell the story put forth by the attorney.[7] For example, Koch Refining Company pled guilty in 1999 to criminal charges of improperly discharging contaminated water and other federal and state environmental violations. The following year a jury returned a verdict in favor of Koch Refining Company in a whistleblower suit brought by Charles Chadwell, a former Koch employee who had alerted regulators to some of these violations. According to the attorney for Chadwell, the case was about the following:

> Mr. Chadwell, a long-term employee with Koch, reported Koch's environmental violations to the Minnesota Pollution Control Agency ("MPCA"), cooperated with MPCA's investigation, and informed Koch that he had done so. Immediately after his first report, Koch began a campaign of harassment and retaliation, subjecting Mr. Chadwell to repeated interrogations, threats, disciplinary measures (including repeated suspensions) and other intimidation tactics intended to punish him for his reports to the MPCA. In December 1997, after more than 20 years of employment with Koch, Mr. Chadwell was terminated.[8]

Chadwell's story closely tracks the elements of proof required under the relevant state whistleblower statute. Mr. Chadwell had to prove that Koch took "adverse employment action" against him because he reported environmental law violations to the state environmental protection regulator.[9]

In defense, Koch argued that Chadwell was fired for failure to cooperate with an internal company investigation of the allegations rather than for reporting the violations. But the narrative presented by the defense in the case focused more on Chadwell's motive for reporting the violations than Koch's motive for firing him. In defending the verdict on appeal, the defense summarized its narrative to the jury:

> The jury did not see Chadwell as a mistreated employee who was punished for doing the right thing. Instead, the jury saw Chadwell as a man who, after Koch turned down his request for a $250,000 "early retirement" package, set out to find some other way to extract a large sum of money from Koch. Chadwell

---

[7] A perhaps extreme example of this phenomena is presented in Professor Dale Carpenter's engrossing book about the landmark decision by the United States Supreme Court holding that criminal sodomy laws violated the Fourteenth Amendment's due process clause. DALE CARPENTER, FLAGRANT CONDUCT: THE STORY OF LAWRENCE V. TEXAS (2012). The narrative of the case presented by the advocacy group attorneys arguing for the accused defendants emphasized the social benefits that flowed from respecting the sexual intimacy of gay citizens. Professor Carpenter shows that the defendants in the suit never engaged in sex on the night of the arrest and thus should have never been arrested even if sodomy laws were constitutionally proper.

[8] Appellant's Brief, Chadwell v. Koch Refining Company LP, 251 F.3d 727 (8th Cir. 2000) (No. 00–2477), 2000 WL 33982621, at *2–3.

[9] Rothmeier v. Investment Advisers, Inc., 556 N.W.2d 590, 592 (Minn. Ct. App. 1996).

embarked on a scheme to get himself fired so that he could charge Koch with violation of the Minnesota Whistleblower Statute.[10]

The defense's narrative was not focused on disputed facts or the most legally relevant information. Instead, Koch was providing a different story about why the parties were before the court. Narrative moves us, whatever our role in decision-making, to want to construe the legally relevant facts in a manner that makes the outcome of a case consistent with our desire to see an intuitively fair resolution of the dispute.[11] The judge or jury is going to decide substantially based on a narrative; the only question for the attorney is whether and how she will participate in the construction of that story.

7.1.3 A SUPREME EXAMPLE OF NARRATIVE

When judges explain their decisions in opinions, they adopt the narratives presented by the attorneys or they create their own stories of the cases before them. Consider an example from a United States Supreme Court decision you may have encountered in studying civil procedure. Personal jurisdiction concerns the power of the court over the defendant named in a lawsuit. In *J. McIntyre Machinery, Ltd. v. Nicastro*, 131 S.Ct. 2780 (2011), the United States Supreme Court decided that New Jersey courts lacked jurisdiction over a British scrap metal machine manufacturer sued by a New Jersey resident who was injured in New Jersey.

The Court fractured in reaching this result. Four justices (Kennedy, Roberts, Scalia and Thomas) in the plurality articulated a new formulation of the personal jurisdiction doctrine that resulted in dismissing the suit for lack of jurisdiction. Two concurring justices (Breyer and Alito) reached the same result using existing case law. Three dissenting justices (Ginsburg, Sotomayor and Kagan) would have found authority for New Jersey courts to adjudicate the case.

Of interest here is how these three factions described the case they were deciding. The totality of the description of the plaintiff's injury by the plurality is as follows: "Robert Nicastro seriously injured his hand while using a metal-shearing machine manufactured by J. McIntyre Machinery, Ltd." *Id.* at 2782. The concurrence makes no mention at all of Mr. Nicastro's injury. "On October 11, 2001, a three-ton metal shearing

---

[10] Appellee's Brief, Chadwell v. Koch Refining Company LP, 251 F.3d 727 (8th Cir. 2000) (No. 00–2477), 2000 WL 33982622, at *3.

[11] Attorneys and commentators use other, related terms to describe the use of narrative in law. Scholars have written extensively about "storytelling" in legal advocacy. *See, e.g.,* Toni M. Massaro, *Empathy, Legal Storytelling and the Rule of Law: New Words, Old Wounds?*, 87 Mich. L. Rev. 2099 (1989). Attorneys will often refer to a "theme" for the case, usually meaning a pithy description of the narrative. A close cousin of narrative is the notion of "framing" a dispute or position.

machine severed four fingers on Robert Nicastro's right hand," begins the dissent's lengthy description of the facts. The dissent adds details such as, "[t]he machine that injured Nicastro, a 'McIntyre Model 640 Shear,' sold in the United States for $24,900 in 1995 . . . and features a 'massive cutting capacity'." *Id.* at 2795.

The descriptions of the defendant and its activities, facts more central to the legal concern at issue, are equally divergent.   The plurality offers a four paragraph summary of the British manufacturer's United States sales activities that can be summarized as follows: the manufacturer sold four of the machines in the U. S. through an independent distributor and attended an annual U.S. trade show held in states other than New Jersey. The concurrence offers a similar, abbreviated factual recitation, and emphasizes that only one of the machines was sold in New Jersey. In the dissent's exhaustive recitation of the manufacturer's sales program, we learn that the manufacturer sells and services the machine throughout the world, that it has attended the U. S. industry trade show for 16 years with the intent to sell machines to "anyone interested in the machine from anywhere in the United States," that New Jersey "has long been a hotbed of scrap-metal businesses," and that the company also sold machines called "Niagara" and "Tardis" and other products in the U. S., among a welter of other details about the company's U. S. activities and its relation to the distributor of the machines in the United States. *Id.* at 2795–98.

The plurality decided a case about a generically described plaintiff injury resulting from use of a machine manufactured by a company that sold a tiny number of these machines in the U.S. through an independent agent. The dissent decided a case about a gruesome injury to Mr. Nicastro (four severed fingers on his right hand) resulting from his use of a three-ton, massive cutting machine sold by a company with a long involvement in selling equipment to the American scrap metal market. Would you find it easier to dismiss the case described by the plurality or dismiss the case described by the dissent?   Narrative matters.

7.2 PERSUADING WHOM?

You don't have to be a law student to know that the breakdown of U. S. Supreme Court justices into groups favoring the injured plaintiff and the business defendant in the *Nicastro* decision is unremarkable.   The politicized, sometimes even partisan, fissure in the highest court is an issue of general public discourse. Less obvious is that judges at every level of the judiciary in every jurisdiction have experience and empathies that lead them to construe the law in favor of certain types of plaintiffs or defendants, or in favor of particular outcomes in certain situations.[12]

Understanding that judges differ in their inclination to empathize with various types of litigants is important because an attorney cannot be a persuasive advocate without understanding whom she is trying to persuade. Part of persuasion is considering how the person to whom the communication is targeted will perceive the communication. Attorneys may change the presentation of the case on a motion or on appeal depending on the judge (or judges) deciding the case. The same, of course, is true of juries. An attorney may tell a different narrative in a given case depending on whether the jury is selected from within the City of Portland, Oregon or from a rural area in east Texas.[13]

Litigators attempt to persuade judges and juries. Yet litigators, and certainly transactional attorneys, also attempt to persuade other actors involved in the case. Attorneys persuade other attorneys, for instance. One way to effectively resolve a case is to persuade the opposing counsel that your view of the law or the facts will prevail, thus making it likely that the opposing counsel will advise settlement to his client on terms that will favor your client.

Attorneys also can obtain more favorable settlements by persuading the opposing party. Attorneys cannot contact the opposing party directly (*see* Section 4.3.1), but attorneys usually have opportunities to speak directly to the opposing party in letters or briefs during a mediation or in negotiations at which the other party is present. In some cases, the opposing counsel will not have fully informed her client about the other side of the case, or the opposing party may not appreciate the power of its opponent's narrative or the willingness of the opponent to reasonably consider both sides of the dispute or transaction.

7.3 POLICY AND RESOURCES

Finally, persuasion requires attention to the constraints placed on the decision-maker by the broader consequences of her decisions and by the resource limits of the decision-making environment. This section offers a brief observation about policy and resource limits as a starting point for awareness of context in persuasion.

---

[12] Judge Richard Posner of the United States Court of Appeals for the Seventh Circuit explains well the limits of conceiving of the law as a fixed set of rules in HOW JUDGES THINK (2008). *See also* Thomas B. Colby, *In Defense of Judicial Empathy*, 96 MINN. L. REV. 1944 (2012).

[13] Attorneys also select forums or engage in pretrial litigation over jurisdiction and venue in order to increase the odds of obtaining a judge and jury more likely to understand and empathize with their client. Attorneys ask questions of jurors in *voir dire* and use challenges to strike jurors based on the same principle—finding decision-makers who are likely to empathize with the attorney's narrative of the case.

7.3.1   POLICY

Put yourself in the position of a trial court judge. The plaintiff has filed a case against two defendants—A and B. Company A is a manufacturer of specialized medical imaging equipment that sells the equipment to medical clinics. Company B supplies a critical component of the equipment to the manufacturer. The plaintiff alleges A violated a specific statutory requirement in its sale of the equipment and that B also is liable under the common law because it knew of the violation and did nothing to stop it. Without knowing the specific conduct at issue or the alleged statute violated or legal basis of the claim, can you see a reason that a judge might be reluctant to allow a suit to proceed against B as opposed to allowing the suit to proceed against A?

The plaintiff is asking the court to find B liable for its failure to act on knowledge of the conduct of a business partner. Asking a court to extend liability to such ancillary actors usually will raise policy concerns. A ruling in favor of the plaintiff on this question may create a de facto policy for when component manufacturers of medical equipment, and perhaps any component manufacturer, will need to investigate concerns about the finished products for which they are supplying parts. Any such ruling will likely result in an appeal that draws protests by the trade industry group that the decision will result in widespread market disruption if not overturned. It is much easier to conceive of a case against A that does not implicate these concerns.

Judicial decisions that have policy implications for a market or for delivery of public services or other endeavors induce judicial caution—for good reason. This observation has at least two implications for persuasive advocacy. First, determine if you want to raise the broader policy questions, if you have a choice about the matter. If you want to avoid the complications that come with a case implicating broader policy concerns, construct your claims or defenses, requested relief or legal reasoning in a way that allows you to argue that the decision you are asking the judge to render will not have substantial consequence outside the ruling in the case. For example, the plaintiff in the above example will need to weigh carefully whether suing company B is worth the complications for the lawsuit. Pay attention to when your arguments are straying into this type of treacherous territory.

Sometimes a party wants to raise policy issues, such as when gay rights advocates sought to establish that sodomy laws were unconstitutional. When you want to bring forth, or cannot avoid, a policy concern, think about how to incorporate policy arguments into the narrative of the case. The plaintiff in the above example might counter company B's policy argument by asserting that failure to hold B liable will provide incentives for companies who uncover violations not to report those violations. If the supporting facts exist or can be gathered, the plaintiff could then build a narrative of the case that portrays the conduct of company B as part of an industry-wide attempt to suppress information about product defects, over-pricing, misleading marketing or whatever public purpose animates the alleged violations.[14]

7.3.2   RESOURCES

Money pervades the practice of law. Some laws are never enforced because there is little chance of an attorney being paid to represent an individual litigant and public enforcement agencies operate under budget or political constraints. Cases go to trial because a party has the money to hire an attorney to pursue any avenue for recourse. Other cases are settled because a party exhausts its ability or willingness to pay for the prosecution or defense of the case.

Time also is a resource constraint on decision-makers. It may be more likely that a transaction will be consummated if the attorney can bring a large company's CEO into the deal. Yet such a CEO will not sit through hours of tedious negotiation of details of any deal that is not "make or break" matter for the company. The attorney representing that company has to manage requests for the limited resource of CEO time.

Litigators encounter time constraints with their client, but they also experience the limited attention that the courts can devote to a particular dispute. An attorney may have worked for months or even years assembling the evidence and arguments that went into a summary judgment motion, but the judge hearing the case probably has a bevy of similar motions on his docket. Effective advocacy requires knowing how to present the case in a way that recognizes the constrained attention of the judge. In part, the use of narrative is a response to time constraints. Narrative is a way for attorneys to communicate quickly the essence of a case.

---

[14] Consider how the construction of narrative in support of a policy argument can lead the attorney back to the need to gather facts. In the above example, the narrative about industry-wide suppression of problems will necessitate a broader search of the relevant industry. Of course, this need leads to questions of whether such information is sufficiently relevant to be admitted for consideration by a court or jury, which is a legal issue. Seeing these connections between law, fact gathering and advocacy will help you make sense of the way that experienced attorneys can sometimes shift quickly between talking about the details of a case or the law and talking about the presentation of the case to decision-makers, because these concerns are inter-related.

CHAPTER 8

DISTRIBUTIVE NEGOTIATION

■ ■ ■

Scholars cleave negotiating into two approaches—distributive and integrative.[1] Distributive negotiations are "win-lose, zero-sum, pure conflict, and competitive. . . in which a gain for one party is a loss for the other and in which each party maximizes (its) own outcome."[2] Desirable or not, that is a fair summation of the situation for many types of litigants, especially those for whom the dispute involves past conduct resulting in a loss and there is no expectation of a future relationship between the parties. Many fields of law involve cases that present mostly or wholly disputes that necessitate distributive negotiation. Personal injury cases almost always are about monetary compensation for past injury. Insurance companies and insureds fight over coverage or loss amounts when a violent storm sweeps though an area.

The theory of distributive negotiations can help attorneys structure their thinking about the application of law to the facts of the case and the needs of the client so the attorneys can better prepare clients for the decisions that need to be made in the negotiating process.[3] This chapter presumes the dispute at issue involves only an allocation of a money loss from past conduct or occurrence, and that the parties have foreclosed options other than continued litigation. Chapter 13 examines creating value through integrative negotiation in a multi-issue context that is not "pure conflict" between litigants or other negotiating parties.

The concept of reservation price is central to understanding distributive negotiation theory. Section 8.1 describes reservation price and focuses on the analysis that an attorney should undertake to help a client establish this price prior to negotiation. Section 8.2 shows how distributive negotiating theory uses reservation price to construct a model for when settlement is possible and the range of possible settlement. Finally, section 8.3 introduces negotiating tactics.

---

[1] Gregory E. Kersten, *Modeling Distributive and Integrative Negotiations. Review and Revised Characterization,* 10 GROUP DECISION & NEGOTIATION 493 (2001).

[2] *Id.* at 500.

[3] Remember that settlement terms are decided by the client, *see* Section 6.3.2.

8.1 RESERVATION PRICE

BATNA, which stands for "Best Alternative to Negotiated Agreement," is a concept widely used in negotiating theory.[4] One way to think of BATNA is that it is the best alternative action to settlement. As applied to the particular problem facing litigators in a distributive negotiation over a money loss, the only realistic alternative usually available to the litigant is continuing the litigation or some other form of binding dispute resolution.[5] In this circumstance, the attorney's job can be seen as working with the client to identify the settlement amount at which continuing the litigation is a preferable option to settlement.[6] This settlement amount has been described as a "reservation price." The plaintiff identifies the least amount of money it would take to provide a release of claims, while the defendant derives a number that represents the most amount of money it would pay to avoid continued litigation that might end in a judgment against it.[7]

The three components the attorney considers in thinking about reservation price are as follows: merits evaluation, litigation costs, and non-monetary considerations. The first three subsections below address each of these components. Section 8.1.4 looks at combining all three components to reach a reservation price.

8.1.1 MERITS EVALUATION

Attorneys bring value to negotiation by knowing the law.[8] Much of the work of this course so far has focused on using legal knowledge to

---

[4] Professor Howard Raiffa introduced this concept to negotiating theory in the early 1980s. THE ART AND SCIENCE OF NEGOTIATION (1982). The concept of BATNA applies to all types of negotiation, not just legal disputes and transactions. BATNA is a way to understand effective negotiating in politics, for instance. The U.S. President has to derive a BATNA in negotiating with the U.S. Congress. *See, e.g.,* Neil Irwin, *'Fiscal Cliff' Talks Will Boil Down To One Obscure Acronym: BATNA,* WASH. POST, Nov. 9, 2012, http://www.washingtonpost.com/business/economy/ fiscal-cliff-talks-will-boil-down-to-one-obscure-acronym-batna/2012/11/09/459b0c34-2a7b-11e2-b4e0-346287b7e56c_story.html.

[5] Of course, the litigant could abandon the litigation rather than settle. Litigants in this position enter settlement at a serious disadvantage. *See* Section 9.1.3 (clients that need to settle will generally make generous initial offers).

[6] Although the text in this section assumes that the negotiating parties have only the choice of settlement or continued litigation, parties in litigation may have options in the form of employing alternative dispute resolution mechanisms, such as an advisory jury. In most cases, the parties entering negotiations at an advanced stage of litigation will have already considered and rejected those options.

[7] BATNA is not always the same as a "bottom line" number, or a "reservation price." In the context of a distributive negotiation over money in a lawsuit, however, it serves essentially the same purpose. BATNA becomes more difficult to conceptualize as the options facing the party become more numerous and malleable than the problem of allocating money loss in litigation. *See* Chapter 12.

[8] In litigation, attorneys have a special position because of their unique right to represent clients in court. Whether attorneys are used in non-litigation negotiations because of legal knowledge or other reasons is a matter of disagreement. *See* Stephen Schwarcz, *Explaining the Value of Transactional Lawyering,* 12 Stan. J.L. Bus. & Fin. 486 (2007) (describing different theories for the value proposition of transactional attorneys).

evaluate the merits of the claims and defenses of the parties as the facts of a case evolve during litigation. When faced with the task of engaging in distributive negotiations, this process of judging the merits of the case takes the concrete form of creating a number that represents the attorney's best guess at that moment as to what the plaintiff is likely to be awarded in the litigation. This evaluation of the case merits requires combining an examination of the plaintiff's probability of prevailing on its liability claim with an examination of the plaintiff's likely recovery if it does prevail on liability.

The merits evaluation process can be precise or more conceptual.[9] An exacting and quantitative method of deriving a reservation price is to create a "decision tree" that assigns a numeric probability of prevailing on each claim or defense at dispositive motion and at trial.[10] Litigation outcome decision trees can become elaborate, with sub-trees and multiple possible outcomes associated with different probability levels.[11] A plaintiff facing a summary judgment motion brought by the defendant might construct the following simple decision tree for estimating the chance of prevailing if the case is litigated through trial:

---

[9] Whether or not the attorney finds a quantitative analysis useful, the question remains as to how to communicate possible outcomes to the client, which is a topic explored in section 11.2.

[10] *See* ROBERT H. MNOOKIN, ET. AL., BEYOND WINNING: NEGOTIATING TO CREATE VALUE IN DEALS AND DISPUTES 108–11 (2000) (describing the use of decision trees in distributive negotiations in litigation).

[11] *See, e.g.,* Marc B. Victor, *Interpreting a Decision Tree Analysis of a Lawsuit*, LITIGATION RISK ANALYSIS (2001), www.litigationrisk.com/Reading%20a%20Tree.pdf

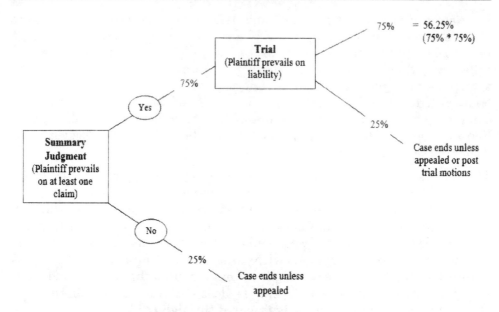

Figure 8–1.

Turning this probability into a dollar amount for purposes of determining reservation price requires that the attorney then make a judgment as to the plaintiff's likely dollar recovery assuming he prevails at trial. Multiplying the percentage chance of prevailing by the estimate of likely recovery yields a dollar value that represents the attorney's best guess as to the value of the case. This amount can be called the "expected value" of the case from the plaintiff's perspective or the "expected cost" from the defendant's perspective.

8.1.2   LITIGATION COSTS

Attorney's fees imposed on clients or concern about future fees often drive many of the choices made by clients in settling litigation. Other litigation costs and risks that commonly impact the determination of reservation price also are noted below.

   * *Attorney's Fees.* Attorney's fees typically are the bulk of litigation expense.   The maxim "it takes money to make money" applies to litigation.   Or, from the defendant's perspective in litigation, it takes money to avoid paying money.

Attorney's fees expended prior to settlement are "sunk costs" and generally should not impact on reservation price, but settling avoids future litigation expense. A rational plaintiff will subtract anticipated future litigation costs, while a rational defendant will add such costs, in determining reservation price because these expenses will not be incurred if the parties settle and thus terminate the litigation.

Some statutes or contracts provide that a prevailing party can recover attorney's fees from the opposing party, or in many cases allow for only one of the parties to recover attorney's fees if it prevails. This condition is known as "fee-shifting," Fee-shifting changes how attorney's fees figure in deriving reservation price.[12] Even in the absence of fee-shifting, the prevailing party in litigation typically is entitled to recover costs—the out-of-pocket expenses of litigation.

* *Time-value of Money.* From the plaintiff's perspective, settlement of litigation brings not only certainty of outcome but also can mean the receipt of money sooner as opposed to recovery in the future.[13] All things being equal, plaintiffs will accept less now rather than a higher amount later.

Some plaintiffs face circumstances that force them to value a payment now at a much higher amount than a future payment. A person unable to work because of injuries may not have enough money to pay their expenses through the course of litigation. This reality has given rise to an industry that finances individuals with certain personal injury or other high value claims.[14] A small business plaintiff may have a hard time generating sufficient cash to continue operations pending an anticipated recovery in litigation.

* *Risk of Recovery.* Experienced attorneys include the potential to recover a judgment as part of the initial case evaluation when the client presents a case involving potential litigation over money loss. A judgment for credit card debt against a consumer with no assets may not be worth the effort. Conversely, a fully insured defendant presents little risk of non-recovery if the plaintiff prevails. Sometimes the litigation itself will influence the evaluation of judgment recovery risk. For example, the complicated history of asbestos litigation in the United States involved claims that would make defendants insolvent if fully recovered.

---

[12] A thorough examination of the impact of fee-shifting on settlement is beyond the scope of this section, but a primary impact is that determining reservation price becomes even more dependent on the chance of success on liability. All reasonable attorneys' fees in the case (past and future) can be treated as part of the likely recovery, with the odds of recovering these fees equal to the odds of prevailing in the case. Similarly, contingency fee arrangements may change the relative interests of the attorney and her client in settlement, as discussed in a wealth of scholarship on the topic. *See, e.g.,* Stephen Daniels & Joanne Martin, *Plaintiff's Lawyer's: Dealing with the Possible but not Certain,* 60 DEPAUL L. REV. 337 (2010).

[13] The potential for the plaintiff to recover pre-judgment interest impacts the consideration of the time-value of money in litigation. Whether the plaintiff in a given suit can obtain pre-judgment interest can be complicated and depend on strategic decisions in litigation as well as the facts of the case. Resolving this question sends the attorney back to legal research that will inform fact gathering and litigation decisions.

[14] *See* Susan Lorde Martin, *The Litigation Financing Industry: The Wild West of Finance Should Be Tamed Not Outlawed,* 10 Fordham J. Corp. & Fin. L. 55 (2004).

8.1.3   NON-MONETARY CONSIDERATIONS

Non-monetary considerations used in deriving a reservation price should always include gauging the client's appetite for risk in the litigation. A plethora of other non-monetary concerns can be important in deriving reservation price.

* *Risk Tolerance.* Several clients facing the exact same situation and provided with the exact same legal analysis are unlikely to reach the same reservation price because those clients will have different tolerance for the risk of litigation. A tolerance for the risk of litigation, or risk-avoidance in litigation, may result from the disposition of the client. One client accused of embezzlement may be willing to take a chance on a trial, while another client facing the same charge and the same estimate of the likelihood of being found guilty at trial will take a plea deal. Or risk tolerance may be a product of the objective circumstances facing the client.

* *Non-monetary Goals.* Section 3.1.1 lists common non-monetary goals of clients. Non-monetary goals may directly influence how the client determines reservation price. An extreme example is when a litigant wants to go to trial to tell his story and all other considerations are secondary, so an impossibly high reservation price is dictated by the non-monetary goal. More typically, the reservation price for monetary recovery will be considered in relation to the non-monetary goals. A government regulator may be willing to settle a case for a civil penalty of $X plus an injunction proscribing certain future conduct, or it may be willing to accept as sufficient deterrence a larger penalty (say, $X*5) without an injunction. Or a defendant may have one reservation price for settling a suit with a confidentiality provision prior to suit, and a lower reservation for settling the dispute after allegations are made public.

Sometimes what appears as risk-taking or risk-avoidance in litigation is dictated by non-monetary goals of the client. The lower-earning parent in a divorce proceeding may be willing to settle for lower maintenance payments because of the harm to the children from continued litigation, but the parent has not or does not want to articulate this concern to the attorney. A company executive may want to settle a case quietly because litigation will expose mismanagement and threaten her pay package. The attorney should be mindful of the distinction between risk preference and these non-monetary factors driving aversion or attraction to litigation. Attorneys who have built trust with the client are more likely to have the client disclose non-monetary goals influencing what might appear to be unusual risk-aversion or risk-taking.

8.1.4   COMBINING THE COMPONENTS OF RESERVATION PRICE

The above factors can be combined to arrive at a reservation price. Consider the following simple example using a quantitative approach to the merits evaluation.

> Merits Evaluation: A plaintiff has a 60% chance of prevailing on liability and has determined that the likely recovery is $50,000 if she prevails. This leads to an expected value of $30,000 ($50,000 * .60).

> Litigation Costs: No fee-shifting is possible in this case and the attorney is working on an hourly fee basis. Attorney's fees and costs currently are $5,000, with expected fees and costs through trial of an additional $15,000. The defendant is profitable and solvent and a judgment would be recoverable, and the plaintiff places little value on a more prompt recovery.

> Putting the above two factors together, a client who is the plaintiff might be expected to set a reservation price of about $15,000 based on a $30,000 expected value minus $15,000 in anticipated future litigation costs saved by settling. A client who is the defendant might be expected to set a reservation price of about $45,000 based on a $30,000 expected cost plus $15,000 in anticipated future litigation costs saved by settling the case. The ZOPA would be between $15,000 and $45,000.

> Non-monetary Factors: Imagine that the dispute at issue involves a suit by a manufacturer against a supplier. The plaintiff is not especially risk-averse or risk-taking. The manufacturer switched suppliers after the dispute arose, but now is dissatisfied with the new supplier and would like to return to using the defendant as a supplier. Perhaps the plaintiff manufacturer would be willing to set a reservation price of less than $15,000 if the settlement could result in re-building goodwill that facilitates a future business relationship between the litigants.

In the above example, all three factors substantially impact the calculation of reservation price. In many cases, however, one factor or another will drive the decision. A client with a strong non-monetary concern may have little use for a merits evaluation or a consideration of litigation costs. More often, the merits evaluation is the critical factor. A claim can be especially valuable when there is a strong likelihood of proving liability and the remedy if successful will result in a high damage award or an otherwise preferable recovery. Conversely, the lowest value case has neither of these characteristics. In either of these situations, the costs and risks associated with litigation will be considered, but the decision on reservation price will more likely be dictated by this evaluation of the merits.

The more difficult cases to value often have either probable liability or high recovery, but not both. In these cases, the costs of litigation and risk tolerance will more likely drive the decision-making as to reservation price. At a general level, the process of determining reservation price from a plaintiff's perspective can be depicted as follows:

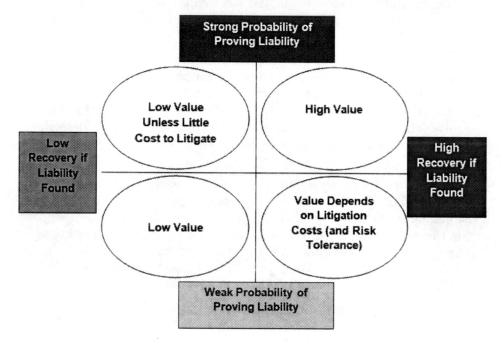

Figure 8–2.

If a party probably can prevail on liability but will recover little by doing so, the cost of litigation becomes a key factor in the decision. If a party is less likely to prevail, but will win a substantial award if successful, the value of the case will depend on the cost of litigating the case and the client's (or the attorney's) tolerance for risk. In other words, the second factor (costs) and the third factor (risk tolerance and non-monetary goals) usually will be more prominent concerns in cases with either a concern over liability or a concern over recovery amount.

Consider an example from the toxic gas release scenario described in Section 2.1.

> The attorney's interview of Ms. McDonald found that she did not suffer any permanent injuries from the gas release, although she spent a few days in the hospital where she experienced physical irritation and stress. Because of the lack of permanent injury, the potential recovery for Ms. McDonald would not be especially

high. Let's assume that the chances of prevailing against Bi-Tell are very good. These assumptions place the case in the upper-left quadrant of the above figure.

An action by Ms. McDonald, then, will depend mostly on the cost of proving liability. If a neighbor of Ms. McDonald was seriously injured by the leaked gas and litigated the case successfully through to a jury trial, perhaps Ms. McDonald could use affirmative issue preclusion on a dispositive motion and prevail without having to conduct discovery or bring the case to trial.[15] Conversely, if no other neighbors suffered permanent injury and only one or two other neighbors have any personal injury claim, then the costs of proving Bi-Tell's negligence, assuming that is necessary, may exceed the small recoveries possible. Or perhaps this is a situation where strict liability may apply and that issue would resolve on a summary judgment motion.

But what if significant punitive damages were a possibility here? This shifts the case to the upper-right quadrant of Figure 1 if the chance of proving liability for punitive damages is high, or the lower-right quadrant if the chance of proving liability for punitive damages is low. In the latter situation—a lesser chance of obtaining a recovery of a large amount of money—it is likely the attorney rather than the client who will have to weigh her tolerance for risk. Most personal injury cases are taken on a contingency fee by the attorney, so the attorney will need to evaluate her willingness to accept the risk of getting little or nothing in this situation versus her expenditure of time and perhaps out-of-pocket expense.

8.2 USING RESERVATION PRICE(S) TO FIND "ZOPA"

The opposing party in litigation also has a reservation price. Negotiating theorists have developed the concept of "ZOPA," or zone of possible agreement, to describe the comparative evaluation of the parties' reservation prices. Section 8.2.1 explains ZOPA, while section 8.2.2 looks at how to estimate ZOPA.

8.2.1   ZOPA

In the context of a distributive negotiation in litigation, ZOPA is the difference between the higher reservation price of the party potentially liable (the defendant) and the lower reservation price of the party seeking

---

[15] "Issue preclusion . . . bars successive litigation of an issue of fact or law actually litigated and resolved in a valid court determination essential to the prior judgment, even if the issue recurs in the context of a different claim." Taylor v. Sturgell, 128 S. Ct. 2161, 2171 (2008).

a monetary recovery in the litigation (the plaintiff). No ZOPA exists if the reservation price of the plaintiff is higher than the reservation price of the defendant.

Consider the suit by Nowecki Dry Cleaners against Clean Chem. Company ("3C") introduced in Section 1.1. Nowecki is seeking a judgment of $90,000 in the suit. Nowecki's attorney advises the dry cleaner that it has a very strong case on the merits, but Nowecki is risk averse, the costs of litigation are a factor, and Nowecki has concerns about 3C's solvency and thus concerns about its recovery of a possible judgment. After evaluating these factors with its attorney, Nowecki determines a reservation price of $55,000.

3C's attorney has a similar evaluation of the case merits and costs, but she is advising 3C that it is unlikely, but "not wholly unreasonable," to project that 3C could survive summary judgment and that a jury would split the difference and award about $45,000. 3C has a reservation price of $70,000. The ZOPA in this case is between $55,000 and $70,000, as depicted in Figure 8-3:

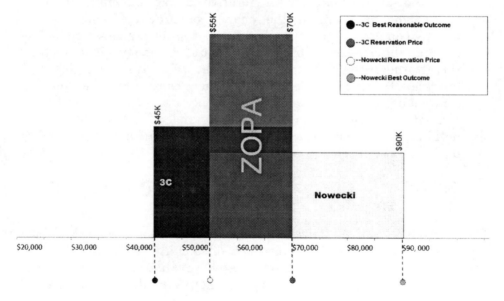

Figure 8–3.

A settlement is possible here because Nowecki has a lower reservation price than 3C. The range for a possible settlement is between $55,000 and $70,000 if both sides maintain their reservation price during the negotiation.

8.2.2　ESTIMATING ZOPA

Knowing the opposing party's reservation price means knowing the ZOPA. If you know the other side's reservation price, you can quickly determine if a settlement is possible and the best terms of settlement for your client. If both sides know each other's reservation price, they would likely agree on settling at the midpoint of the ZOPA, if it exists. Barring unusual circumstances, these situations will not occur. Instead, the parties are left with the task of trying to estimate each other's reservation price. This subsection discusses factors to consider in estimating ZOPA.[16]

Start estimation of the opponent's reservation price by conducting the same case valuation process from the perspective of the other party. In other words, look at the merits, litigation costs and non-monetary concerns from the opponent's point of view.

*　Merits Evaluation.* The likelihood of two rational parties settling litigation depends substantially on whether the opposing attorneys have a comparable evaluation of the merits of the case. Parties holding significantly discrepant and self-interested conclusions about the merits of the case based on consultation with their attorneys are less likely to determine reservation prices that overlap. If 3C's attorney had advised her client that 3C was likely to prevail on summary judgment or at trial, 3C would probably have a reservation price lower than $55,000 and settlement would not occur.

Research suggests that attorneys engaged in litigation, both civil and criminal, routinely overestimate the likelihood of succeeding in litigation.[17] This overconfidence bias may result in prolonged litigation by making it impossible or difficult for the parties to settle.

More importantly for purposes of estimating the other side's reservation price, the parties to litigation may have asymmetric information. Prior to disclosure and discovery, it is often the case that each side has access to information that is not available to the other side. For this reason, it is sometimes difficult settle a case before discovery because each side, and usually especially the plaintiff, has to estimate chances of success by conjecturing about what information might be produced in discovery, thus

---

[16] Section 9.1.4 discusses how estimates of the other side's reservation price, and thus estimates of ZOPA, impact initial offer amounts in litigation.

[17] Jane Goodman-Delahunty, et al., *Insightful or Wishful: Lawyers' Ability to Predict Case Outcomes*, 16 PSYCHOL., PUB. POL'Y, & L. 133 (2010) (reporting results of a large-scale study showing that attorneys in both civil and criminal cases regularly show overconfidence as to the likelihood of achieving minimum goals and cataloguing prior studies of the subject showing a similar result). Gender, but not experience, correlates with overconfidence. The study authors concluded that, "female lawyers were susceptible to the overconfidence bias only when the predicted likelihood of success was high. Compared with their female colleagues, male lawyers were less able to discriminate between cases in which they had a moderate probability of success (65–75%) and those in which they had a high probability of success (over 75%)." *Id.* at 143

making it harder for even scrupulously objective attorneys to reach the same evaluation of the merits.

Settlement becomes more likely as litigation progresses. Discovery should put the parties in a similar position as to the knowledge of the facts. Motion rulings by the judge provide the parties with determinations that lessen, if not remove, the uncertainty as to the legal validity of the plaintiff's claims and defenses. Each stage of the litigation removes uncertainty and thus should prompt the opposing parties to adopt a more uniform evaluation of the merits.

     * *Litigation Costs.* In the absence of fee-shifting, litigation costs should compel most rational parties advised by objective attorneys to settle. If the two parties have a similar evaluation of the merits of the case, and non-monetary factors are not substantially influencing decision-making, the vast majority of such cases should settle if both parties are behaving rationally. The fact that both parties are facing future attorney's fees should drive the plaintiff's reservation price down and the defendant's reservation price up, thus creating a ZOPA. Estimating the other side's attorney's anticipated future fees allows an attorney to move the other side's reservation price in a favorable direction.

     * *Non-monetary Considerations.* Factors not susceptible to an objective evaluation of monetary consequence often move the parties toward or away from settlement. These factors may be expressly stated or apparent. For example, a company under investigation by a government regulator almost always will fear how negative publicity about its business could cause adverse reactions by consumers, investors or other participants in the industry. This concern can lead the government to raise the reservation price of the target company in settlement negotiations prior to suit. Companies that can announce a settlement rather than face a public announcement of a lawsuit can present the settlement as resolving the regulator's concerns and eliminate the uncertainty about the company's operations that might be engendered by a lawsuit.

Other non-monetary factors will not be obvious to the opposing party. An attorney may be able to make an evaluation of the other side's concerns based on research into its past conduct or signals in the litigation. Return to the example of a government regulator investigating a company for violations of the law enforced by the regulator. The regulator can attempt to gauge the preference of the company for litigation risk by looking into how it has handled past regulatory concerns, by determining the vulnerability of the company to reputational concerns or by taking into account whether the company hires a lead attorney to defend it who is known for generating settlements or known for aggressive litigation tactics.

8.3 BARGAINING BASICS

Negotiating skills of attorneys also can impact the chances of settlement and where the settlement occurs within the range defined by the ZOPA. In the Nowecki example, if both negotiators are equally skilled and the clients are equally rational, the parties can be expected to distribute the $15,000 surplus evenly and settle for $62,500. If the attorneys are not equally skilled, the case may not settle or it may settle for closer to either $55,000 or $70,000. This section briefly notes skill-building issues in negotiation. Some of the key topics presented here are discussed in more depth later in this text.

Start with an example. Maleek is trying to sell a car he bought for $19,000 about three years ago. Maleek has advertised the sale price as $14,000. He has an offer from a used car dealer to buy the vehicle for $10,000, which he will take if he cannot sell it through his ad (i.e., Maleek's reservation price in negotiating theory terms). Justine takes the car on a test drive and then to her mechanic for an evaluation of the car's mechanical condition, which is positive. Then Justine and Maleek begin to bargain.

Justine: I will give you $6,000 for the car.

Maleek: I can't sell this car for anywhere near $6,000. But you can have it for $11,000. That's my best price on it.

Justine: I only have $9,000 to spend on a car. I can give you a cashier's check today for that amount.

Maleek: Well, it would be nice to sell it today, so why don't we split the difference and you give me $10,000 for the car.

Justine: My aunt can probably float me the difference. I'll call her.

Justine will no doubt complete the purchase of the car for Maleek's reservation price, which is the best possible deal she could have arranged in this situation. What would you do differently in negotiating with Justine if you could appear on the scene and act as Maleek's attorney? Below are common concerns facing attorneys engaged in distributive negotiations

Anchoring, Ranges, and Initial Offers. The initial offer by each side usually sets expectations for the negotiation. The concept of initial offers as anchoring expectations and the related notion of signaling a range for possible settlement are discussed in Section 9.1.

Settlement That Achieves Goals versus Achieving the Goal of Settlement. The purpose of negotiation is not to reach a settlement—it is to reach a settlement that improves the client's position. A pre-determined reservation price helps negotiators to avoid the common problem of seeing settlement as the purpose of negotiation rather than a possible result of negotiation. Knowing a reservation price before negotiating grounds the attorney and the client to a floor (or ceiling) for an acceptable settlement outcome. If the client agrees to a deal in negotiation that is worse than the pre-determined reservation price, obtaining a settlement did not improve the client's position, assuming that no new, reliable information was revealed that would change your client's evaluation of the case.

Parties (and attorneys) can become irrationally committed to accomplishing a settlement for the sake of justifying the time spent in negotiation. There is almost always an opportunity to walk away from settlement discussions that do not achieve an acceptable result. This obviously does not preclude the parties from re-starting negotiations at a later date after developments have occurred or the parties have obtained more information.

Movement and Rationale. After the initial offers, both sides will need to make further offers if the negotiations are to continue. These offers communicate specific terms on which each side will settle, but these offers also signal to the opposing side eagerness to settle and willingness to make further concessions. In the above example, Maleek quickly nose-dived from the advertised price of $14,000 to an offered sales price of $11,000. He did so with no explanation of why he would make such a quick concession. Similarly, Justine matched this counter-offer by also adding $3,000, or 50%, to his initial offer price of $6,000. Both sides are signaling with these offers that they want a quick deal and that they had little rationale for their initial offers. Interpreting concession patterns in negotiations is discussed in detail in Section 11.3.

Other Bargaining Tactics and Responses. Once the back and forth of negotiation begins, you may encounter one or more of the following common tactics.

> (1) <u>Flinch</u>. An initial offer by one side is met with surprise, immediate rejection or even a physical "flinch" from the other side. This may be an honest reaction to an unrealistic offer. It could have been appropriate for Maleek to flinch at a $6,000 offer on a car he had listed for $14,000. Or a flinch can be a calculated tactic. A flinch signals, genuinely or not, that the offer does not imply a range for settlement that will make agreement possible.

> (2) <u>External Limits/Commitment</u>. A stereotype car dealer negotiating tactic is to say something like, "I would love to offer you the car for that price, but I know my manager and he will say I can't go any lower." Confronted with this type of defense to considering an offer, an attorney can ask that the opposing

counsel consult his client, and clarify that the represented position of the client is truly inflexible.

(3) <u>"Take-it or Leave-it" Ultimatum</u>. A related and well-known tactic is "bottom line" language; e.g., "this is my last offer, take-it or leave-it." One response can be to just ignore an ultimatum and negotiate as if it were not uttered. Or a party that does not believe the ultimatum is the best deal possible may sever the current negotiations and continue litigation in the hope that a more favorable result will be reached through continued litigation.

(4) <u>Post-settlement Nibbles</u>. An especially annoying tactic can be the "nibble"—a suggestion to alter the deal after it appears that the parties have reached a settlement. Sometimes a nibble is a small item that a party will accede to in order to preserve the deal. A way to mitigate this problem is to reduce the deal to writing as soon as agreement is reached between the parties, or to make clear at the time of negotiation that all issues have been resolved by the settlement.

CHAPTER 9

WRITTEN SETTLEMENT OFFERS IN DISTRIBUTIVE NEGOTIATION

■ ■ ■

Negotiation often starts with a letter.[1] Parties in litigation usually will exchange written communication before or after in-person negotiation. An initial letter to an opposing party (or opposing counsel if the party is known to be represented) setting forth proposed settlement terms in lieu of initiating litigation is known as a "demand letter."

This chapter examines both the substance and style of written settlement offers, with a continued focus on distributive negotiation in litigation over past money loss. An important decision facing the attorney and client in drafting a settlement offer is determining the amount of the offer. Section 9.1 looks at "anchors" and "ranges" in settlement negotiations, and discusses how these concepts can be used to determine the amount of an initial settlement offer in cooperation with the client. Section 9.2 applies the basic principles of advocacy and negotiation to the task of writing an effective settlement offer letter. Finally, Section 9.3 consists of two sample written settlement offer letters—an initial offer and a response to that offer.

9.1 DETERMINING INITIAL SETTLEMENT OFFER AMOUNT

Valuing a case should be an objective process that leads to communication with the client about setting a reservation price and a framework for settlement negotiations. Determining an amount for an initial settlement offer in distributive negotiations in litigation introduces a new set of variables. This subsection describes the concepts and concerns that inform working with the client to arrive at an initial offer amount.[2]

---

[1] Or email or other form of electronic communication, of course. Even in the second decade of the 21st century, however, attorneys often use formal letters to communicate settlement offers and responses, even if those letters are transmitted electronically.

[2] The simulation in this course assigns one of the parties the task of making the first offer and the other party the task of responding to that offer. The question of whether to make the first offer is another matter of importance at the outset of negotiations. *See* STEFAN H. KRIEGER & RICHARD K. NEUMANN, JR., ESSENTIAL LAWYERING SKILLS: INTERVIEWING, COUNSELING, NEGOTIATION, AND PERSUASIVE FACT ANALYSIS 355–56 (4th ed. 2011).

9.1.1   ANCHORS AND RANGES

Daniel Kahneman and Amos Tversky, Stanford Professors of Psychology who study human judgment and decision-making, have shown that an initial "anchor" amount can influence decision-making.   In one well-known experiment, Kahneman and Tversky spun a wheel to derive a random number for two groups of subjects. The first group saw the wheel produce the number 10, while the second group saw the wheel produce the number 65.   The two groups were then asked to estimate the percentage of African countries in the United Nations. The group that saw the wheel produce the number 10 estimated that 25% of the U. N. countries were African, while the group that saw the wheel turn up the number 65 estimated the percentage of African countries as 45%.[3]

The initial settlement offer is an anchor in legal negotiations.   It can serve to influence the perception of the negotiating parties as to a feasible outcome.   Attorney Dan Orr and Professor Chris Guthrie reviewed a wide range of studies on negotiating and concluded that "anchoring has a powerful influence on negotiation outcomes," and that this observation is only partly qualified when considering more experienced negotiators and those with greater access to information about the dispute.[4] Anchoring works by setting expectations of value and thus setting the range of possible outcomes in the negotiation. It is common that parties will settle somewhere about halfway between their initial offers, thus making the initial anchoring offers critical to the outcome in many cases.

Professor Charles Craver describes an example of anchoring in a law school class exercise he performs each year:

> I ask each student to answer two questions. First, how much would they include in their initial offer? Second, how much do they think they will have to pay to resolve this law suit? Although the students all receive the identical factual information, one critical factor is different. Half are told that the plaintiff counsel has just demanded $100,000 and half are told counsel has just demanded $50,000. The students facing the $100,000 demand plan higher opening offers than the students facing the $50,000 demand. The students facing the $100,000 demand also indicate that they expect to pay more to resolve the matter than the students facing the $50,000 demand.[5]

---

[3] Amos Tversky and Daniel Kahneman, *Judgment under Uncertainty: Heuristics and Biases*, 185 SCIENCE 1124, 1128 (1974).

[4] Dan Orr & Chris Guthrie, *Anchoring, Information, Expertise and Negotiation: New Insights from Meta-Analysis*, 21 OHIO ST. J. ON DISP. RESOL. 597, 624 (2006).

[5] Charles B. Craver, *What Makes A Great Legal Negotiator?*, 56 LOY. L. REV. 337, 353–54 (2010).

9.1.2   CREDIBLE OFFERS

So why not make a ridiculously high initial offer? The initial offer should be as high as possible while also being credible. If you are selling an average two bedroom home in a community in which such homes sell for about $200,000, advertising a price of $500,000 for the home will depress, or entirely eliminate, the number of people willing to look at the home. If a party makes an initial demand of $1 million in settlement, and then collapses to an offer of $100,000 when the opposing party refuses to counter-offer, the $1 million offer obviously does not serve the purpose of establishing an anchor in the negotiation, and the party making the offer loses credibility in the negotiating process.

For parties making an offer intended to start serious negotiations toward settlement, the goal of the initial offer is to communicate a credible amount that signals your client's belief in the strength of his case. Assuming that a settlement is possible given the respective case valuations and goals of the parties, a credible offer usually will be just enough to make the opposing party decide that a settlement might be achieved given that party's reservation price, but no more than the amount necessary to create that impression.

9.1.3   SETTLEMENT URGENCY

So does that mean an initial settlement offer that makes the opposing party walk away from the negotiations is too high? Not necessarily, depending on the client's urgency to settle and the timing of the settlement offer in the litigation. It is rarely to anyone's advantage to make an offer knowing that the opposing party will consider it unworthy of a response. Yet a party that is willing to continue the litigation and is confident of its chance of success may not be especially concerned about having the opposing party walk away from possible negotiations due to an aggressive settlement offer. A party may want to make a show of strength with an aggressive offer to signal something other than the start of serious negotiation efforts; for instance, demonstrating that the party making the offer is prepared to litigate through to trial.

This is especially true if the settlement offer occurs at an earlier point in pretrial litigation. For instance, if the offer occurs before anticipated dispositive motions are decided, there will be later opportunities to re-start negotiations from a better (or worse) position after the court's ruling on the motion. At that time, there will be a clear reason for one party to change its bargaining position.

Conversely, clients that need to settle lose leverage in negotiation, and that loss of leverage likely will appear in the initial offer. A client needing to settle a case immediately will want to make sure the initial offer keeps the opposing party engaged in the negotiation. If an overriding objective for the attorney is to achieve the client's goal of a rapid settlement, the attorney would likely recommend an initial offer amount that reflects a very conservative evaluation of the opposing party's willingness to walk away from the offer—in other words, an initial settlement offer that is lower from the plaintiff or higher from the defendant than it otherwise would be if there was no urgency to settle. A conservative offer would more likely result in continued negotiation toward settlement than would an aggressive offer.

9.1.4   THE IMPORTANCE OF ESTIMATING ZOPA

As described in Section 8.2, negotiations with rational parties will only be successful if there is a ZOPA—a zone of possible agreement representing an overlap between the parties' reservation prices. Attorneys try to estimate the opposing party's reservation price in order to estimate whether a ZOPA might exist and the range of that ZOPA. If the goal of the initial offer amount is to make a credible offer that is just enough to lead the opposing party to imagine negotiations that will at least meet its reservation price, then making a guess as to the opposing party's reservation price is a necessary component of determining a credible initial offer amount.

Mistakes in estimating that price can be costly. An initial offer by a defendant of more than the plaintiff's reservation price, or even very close to the price, leaves the plaintiff with leverage to push as far as possible toward the edge of the ZOPA defined by the defendant's reservation price. An initial offer that is far below the opposing party's reservation price runs the risk of prematurely ceasing negotiations.

Consider again the Nowecki litigation against 3C. Nowecki has demanded $90,000 in the Complaint and imagine now that Nowecki's attorney has sent 3C's attorney a letter offering to settle the litigation for $83,000. 3C's attorney, of course, does not know that Nowecki's reservation price is $55,000. 3C has a reservation price of $70,000. Think about two scenarios for 3C's response:

> Scenario A. 3C's attorney determines that Nowecki has little reason to compromise because of its strong position on the merits of the case and thus its likely reservation price is about the same as 3C, around $70,000. Accordingly, 3C's attorney recommends to 3C an initial offer of $50,000 ("Counter-offer A" in the chart below), which 3C's attorney suggests is just enough to lead Nowecki to believe that the case can be settled.

> Scenario B. 3C's attorney concludes that Nowecki is concerned about litigating with a larger company and is very risk-averse, and thus it likely has a reservation price around $40,000.

Accordingly, 3C's attorney recommends to 3C that its initial offer be $20,000 ("Counter-offer B" in the chart below).

The initial Nowecki offer and the 3C offer under each of the above two scenarios can be graphed as follows:

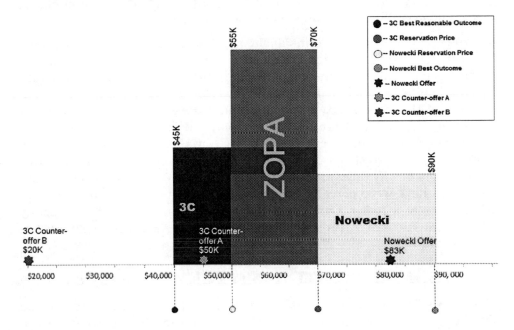

Figure 9–1.

Offer A over-estimates Nowecki's reservation price. Considered next to the Nowecki offer, Offer A puts the range between the two "anchor" offers as $50,000–$83,000. If the parties negotiate a splitting of the difference, the settlement will be $66,500, near the top end of the ZOPA for Nowecki and almost at 3C's $70,000 reservation price.

Offer B under-estimates Nowecki's reservation price. If the parties split this difference, the result will be $51,500, under Nowecki's reservation price of $55,000. Is this offer so low that Nowecki will walk away from the negotiations? Probably not. But if Nowecki's reservation price really was $70,000, as imagined by 3C's attorney in scenario A, a $20,000 offer may have terminated negotiations. As noted above, 3C may or may not be especially concerned about Nowecki walking away from negotiations at this point.

9.1.5 NEGOTIATING NORMS

It is easy to imagine showing the above reading to an experienced attorney and having her say, "That's not how attorneys I know go about settlement. We make a fair guess at the value of the case, perhaps shaded up or down a bit based on our client's perspective, and then usually just reach a deal pretty quickly." Or an experienced attorney may have the opposite view based on her experience, and advise that all initial offers from plaintiffs should be exorbitant and all initial offers from defendants should be minimal. And these attorneys would no doubt be accurately describing their legal practice.

Attorneys have different norms about negotiation depending on the type and setting of the practice. Professor Herbert Kritzer, for example, studied negotiating style among personal injury attorneys in five different jurisdictions and concluded that "the mode of negotiation may . . . be a function of the 'community of negotiators.'"[6] Negotiation norms vary by geography. A study of family law attorneys in lightly populated Maine found that negotiations were characterized by cooperation and attention to presenting offers that would be seen as reasonable and credible, while a survey of family law practitioners in Chicago and Milwaukee found these attorneys were perceived to be comparatively more aggressive than other types of attorneys and "had the highest percentage of unethically adversarial lawyers."[7] As with every aspect of legal practice, conduct is contextual.

9.2 COMMUNICATING SETTLEMENT OFFERS

Written settlement offers should be specific as to amount and terms and should provide a rationale for the offer. The appropriate length, tone, level of detail and content of the letter depends on the context in which the letter is sent, but should reflect an understanding of some basic principles for effectively framing settlement offers. This section examines the following four concepts to consider when drafting a settlement letter: specificity, rationale, context, and framing.

9.2.1   SPECIFICITY

A settlement offer should be specific about the terms of the proposed settlement. There is little point in sending a settlement offer letter asking for "substantial damages" or "an injunction that will prevent the type of conduct that led to this dispute." These types of requests do not move negotiations forward because they do not require the opposing party to respond with a specific offer or at least reject a specific amount or term. Ambiguous offers can signal a lack of confidence in or understanding of the case on the part of the attorney or his client. A credible offer is a specific offer.

---

[6] HERBERT M. KRITZER, LET'S MAKE A DEAL: UNDERSTANDING THE NEGOTIATION PROCESS IN ORDINARY LITIGATION 129 (1991).

[7] *Compare* LYNN MATHER ET AL., DIVORCE LAWYERS AT WORK: VARIETIES OF PROFESSIONALISM IN PRACTICE (2001) *with* Andrea Kupfer Schneider & Nancy Mills, *What Family Law Attorneys are Really Doing When They Negotiate*, 44 FAM. CT. REV. 612, 617 (2006).

Try to be specific as to consequence when possible. Specificity in offers should extend to a description of the actions that the offeror will take, or the consequences that will result for the offeree, if the offer is rejected or ignored. A generic threat of initiating litigation or continuing to trial can seem as impotent as a generic request for "substantial damages." As Professors Krieger and Neumann write, a settlement offer that vaguely indicates that the attorney is "going to take this case to trial" can appear as if "she is going through the motions of stating a consequence, rather than developing one persuasively."[8] Instead of generally threatening litigation, the attorney usually should state specific claims with specific damage demands that will result if the attorney must resort to filing a claim. Instead of generally threatening a certain type of motion or intent to proceed to trial, the attorney usually should paint a picture of the contents of that motion or trial as an event that the opposing party will want to avoid. Specific consequences will more likely motivate action.

Similarly, a settlement offer letter should state a date for an expected response or a date the offer will terminate. Think about sending a pre-suit demand letter on September 1 without a date by which the author of the letter will file suit if the offeree fails to respond. What happens if the offeree is silent on September 15, on October 1 or even on October 15? The offeror attorney could call the offeree or its attorney, but that can make the offeror seem desperate for settlement, resulting in a loss of leverage. The offeree could file suit, but it would be hard to know when to assume that the other side will not respond to the offer, thus necessitating the initiation of litigation to keep the case moving forward. Stating in the written settlement offer a specific date for an expected response and the specific consequence that will result if no response is received will prevent this problem.

Specificity as to offer terms is not a goal, however, in some settlement letters. A common example is an attorney responding to an initial settlement offer from the other side when the attorney's client has decided to not make a counter-offer. The attorney's goal in writing such a responsive letter is to demonstrate confidence in the client's position in the matter. One way to think about a letter refusing to make a counter-offer is that it establishes that the initial offer from the other side does not constitute a legitimate anchor for settlement negotiations. An attorney can use this letter to articulate a rationale for the non-response and should pay attention to context and framing, as discussed below. But specificity of offer terms obviously is not necessarily a goal when writing a letter refusing to counter-offer.

---

[8] KRIEGER & NEUMANN, *supra* note 2, at 359.

9.2.2   RATIONALE

Settlement offers and counter-offers should be supported by a reason that the offeree should accede to the demands. A good starting point for thinking about reasons to support a demand is to review Section 8.1 concerning three factors used to derive a reservation price.

Merits. Written settlement offers usually will highlight the merits of the case, both as to liability and remedy. Settlement letters present the case merits because that is a critical reference point for the parties' mutual evaluation of outcome probabilities and thus for rationally valuing the case. Emphasizing favorable facts or law on the merits is a means of stressing your confidence in a high (or low) valuation of the case.

Costs/Risks of Litigation. Almost all settlement offer letters will mention avoidance of the costs and/or risks of litigation as a reason for making a particular settlement offer. Because this factor is a generic advantage of settlement, try also to articulate specific costs and risks that can be avoided by one or both parties through settlement. For instance, if the court's trial schedule is backed up to three years from case filing, a defendant can cite this fact as a means of emphasizing that the plaintiff will not see any possible recovery for years, thus increasing the costs of litigation and the date of any recovery for that party. Or if neither side has yet identified experts, the attorney can point out the substantial cost savings from not having expert testimony as an example of cost savings from settlement.

Non-monetary Factors. In some cases, a central reason to settle is one or more non-monetary goals of the parties. A good example of this situation is a dispute in which at least one of the parties is hoping to settle the matter in order to preserve a positive relationship between the parties. For example, if 3C is hoping to settle its suit with Nowecki by retaining the account, 3C might want to include in its settlement offer letter responding to Nowecki something like the following: "My client is interested in pursuing settlement in this case substantially because 3C hopes to return as an important supplier to Nowecki Dry Cleaners. 3C has worked hard to be a reliable and value-oriented business partner with Nowecki. This letter outlines a proposal for settling the current litigation so that both parties can move forward and benefit from a continuing business relationship."

While settlement letters typically present the merits of the case from the point of view of the party drafting the letter, it is important to understand that a settlement letter is not the same as a legal brief submitted in support of or opposition to a motion. It is sometimes appropriate, but not necessary, to cite legal authority or the record in the case. A settlement letter that mimics a brief risks making arguments that prematurely inform the other party of the specific strategy and information possessed by the offeror. The written settlement offer should reveal new facts unknown to the other side or make new legal arguments only if the attorney has carefully considered how inclusion of this information will bolster the settlement position of the client. A settlement letter is an opportunity to highlight key points, legal or factual, that are persuasive but do not reveal all important details of the offering party's case or settlement position.

9.2.3   CONTEXT

As with most work of an attorney, context will dictate much about how the settlement offer letter should be drafted. Of the many contextual factors that should be considered, two factors often will be of particular importance—when the letter is sent and the intended audience.[9]

When. The length, tone and rationale articulated in a settlement letter will vary with the point in the litigation process at which the letter is sent. A demand letter sent prior to filing suit will usually be longer and more detailed than a settlement offer sent during the course of litigation. The recipient of the pre-suit letter presumably will not have had the benefit of a Complaint or other filings or discussions that identify the key factual allegations and the legal claims of the plaintiff. A settlement letter sent following an unsuccessful mediation and then a summary judgment order may be quite brief, as the parties would have fully aired the merits of the claims and their settlement positions, so the settlement letter likely would focus on the specific terms of an offer more than the persuasive rationale for the offer. The information necessary to identify the basis for the demand and influence the thinking of the opposing party will depend on the prior exchange of information in litigation and the decisions facing the parties at the moment.

Who. In a case with two represented parties, settlement letters will be addressed to counsel for the opposing party.[10] A persuasive settlement letter can have an impact on opposing counsel. A letter that articulates the merits of a claim can influence the opposing counsel's view of the probability of prevailing on the merits, perhaps because the letter integrates the facts and law in a way that demonstrates that the case can

---

[9] Legal context also can be important in the timing and content of the offer letter. Settlement offers can have consequences in litigation, including impacting the shifting of litigation costs to the losing party, creating the potential for later "bad faith" claims in insurance litigation, and allowing for (or preventing) the accrual of pre-judgment interest on claims. Sometimes pre-suit demand letters are a prerequisite to bringing certain types of claims.

[10] To do otherwise would violate Rule 4.2 of the Model Rules of Professional Conduct. *See* Section 4.3.1.

be formed into an effective narrative on motion or at trial. Or the letter may offer a particularly convincing rationale for settlement not previously considered by the opposing attorney. The audience for a written settlement offer, however, may be broader.

Settlement letters should be drafted with an eye to the impact of the letter on a decision-maker in the matter. As discussed in Chapter 6, attorneys are required to share settlement offers with their clients. In many cases, the attorney will do so by forwarding the settlement offer letter to the client. This letter is an opportunity, perhaps even the first opportunity, for the attorney writing the letter to influence directly the opposing party's view of the case. Written settlement offers also can become part of the record in the case, or otherwise come to the attention of the judge, arbitrator or mediator. Attorneys should not write a settlement letter if they would be embarrassed to see it presented to the court or in alternative dispute resolution.

9.2.4 FRAMING

The style of a settlement letter will depend on the attorney drafting the letter. Some attorneys are bellicose. Some attorneys rely on formulaic presentations in every case. Attorneys vary tremendously in style and approach as people vary tremendously in style and approach. Yet there are useful notions for any attorney to consider in drafting a written settlement offer, including the three concepts discussed below.

Gain Framing. Presenting settlement as a gain for the other side rather than as avoidance of a loss can improve the odds of the opposing party preferring settlement to continued litigation. Empirical research has shown that "[w]hen people choose among potential gains, they tend to be risk-averse, but when they choose among potential losses, they tend to be risk-seeking."[11] This research argues for framing settlement offers as gains when possible, if the goal is to actually obtain a settlement.

Cooperative Tone. Presenting a cooperative attitude in making a written settlement offer makes it more likely for the opposing party to want to complete a deal. This is common sense, but also a command easy to forget in sharply contested litigation. The most difficult obstacle to settlement often is the hardened attitudes of mistrust and anger that arise from contentious behavior. Professor Carrie Sperling describes this reality as follows: "although a lawyer could expect the recipient of a demand letter to take a self-interested position at the outset of a

---

[11] Jeffrey J. Rachlinski, *Gains, Losses, and the Psychology of Litigation,* 70 S. Cal. L. Rev. 113, 123 (1996). Professor Rachlinski's article reviews both experimental tests and data collected in studies of actual litigation behavior that support this conclusion. The psychological research explaining this phenomenon is rooted in the same theory that underlies the concept of "anchors" as impacting settlement, which is the "prospect theory" associated with Professors Daniel Kahneman and Amos Tversky.

negotiation, once the recipient becomes angry and defensive, the likelihood of efficient resolution becomes remote."[12]

For example, avoid hyperbole and aggressive statements, such as "Simchek is wasting my client's time and money with the frivolous issues it is raising in this case." Of course, there may be cases in which presenting a brusque tone of affront is appropriate and useful. The above sentence might be appropriate if it is part of a defendant's response to a settlement demand where the defendant states that it will not pay anything in settlement and intends to bring a sanction motion under Fed. R. Civ. P. 11 if the plaintiff fails to voluntarily dismiss the Complaint. But it is probably best to default to a cooperative tone unless there is a compelling reason to take a different approach.

A cooperative tone does not include admitting weaknesses in the case. As Professor Charles Calleros advises as to demand letters:

> A demand letter is not the proper place to make concessions or admissions that may come back to haunt you later. Therefore, if you choose to adopt a conciliatory tone, do so in a way that does not preclude you from taking a stronger position in the future. For example, suppose that your client demands compensation on the basis of a strong contract claim and a weak tort claim. To maintain credibility and to avoid antagonizing the opposing party, you might only invoke the contract claim to justify your client's demands...If so, you should remain silent about the weaker tort claim or refer to it only vaguely.[13]

Re-Framing in Response Letters. One of the most common mistakes made by young attorneys in drafting responses to settlement offers is addressing each point raised in the initial letter and accepting the terms of discussion as presented by the opposing attorney. For example, if a demand letter from an attorney representing a client with an injury emphasizes the details of the client's injuries, her medical expenses and her emotional suffering, it may be appropriate not to discuss any of these details in the response letter if the primary defense is lack of proof of negligence. The responsive letter should present the narrative from the point of view of the client responding and focus on the matters and facts of consequence to that party's position. There is no need to respond to every point raised by the opposing party. This often is good advice for a motion brief, but it is especially true in the beginning negotiation dance that is typical of written settlement offer letters.

---

[12] Carrie Sperling, *Priming Legal Negotiations Through Written Demands*, 60 CATH. U. L. REV. 107, 120 (2010). *See also* Bret Rappaport, *A Shot Across the Bow: How to Write an Effective Demand Letter*, 5 J. ASS'N LEGAL WRITING DIRECTORS 32 (2008).

[13] CHARLES R. CALLEROS, LEGAL METHOD AND WRITING 526 (5th ed. 2006).

This process of re-framing in a responsive written settlement letter is analogous to the concept of anchoring. The attorney drafting the responsive letter should not let the initial letter set the boundaries of discussion for the settlement. The responsive letter, like the responsive money offer, sets that party's anchor for the matters that should dominate the settlement discussions.

9.3 EXEMPLAR SETTLEMENT OFFER LETTERS

This section provides an example of a settlement offer letter by the attorney for Nowecki to the attorney for 3C, and a response to that offer letter by 3C's attorney. These are samples of a wide variety of styles and approaches that can be used in drafting a settlement offer letter.

9.3.1 NOWECKI OFFER LETTER

September 28, 2012

Cheryl Houghton
Mickey, Katzen and Tesker, P.A.
1706 Welton Street
Denver, CO 80201

Re: Rule 408 Confidential Settlement Offer[14] in *Nowecki Dry Cleaning, Inc. v. CleanChem Company,* Court File No. 12–cv–035

Dear Ms. Houghton:

I am writing with a settlement offer that hopefully will obviate the need for the upcoming mediation scheduled for November 7, 2012 and save both parties further litigation expense. Nowecki Dry Cleaners will dismiss its suit and provide 3C with a complete release of all claims in this case for a payment by 3C of $83,000.

The facts in this case are neither complicated nor in dispute. On December 2, 2010, Nowecki and 3C agreed to a three-year supply contract under which 3C was obligated to provide the dry cleaning chemical parthaethyml ("Parth") to Nowecki at $50 per pound for the period January 1, 2010 through December 31, 2012. 3C expressly and materially breached that contract in its letter to Nowecki dated December 29, 2011 by declaring that it would no longer sell Parth to Nowecki at the contractual price of $50 per pound.

The $50 per pound price was in excess of the current market price at the time the parties agreed to the supply contract. Nowecki nonetheless entered the supply contract with 3C to ensure price stability for its

---

[14] Evidentiary rules provide that settlement offers cannot be introduced for the purpose of proving "the validity or amount of a disputed claim" or to impeach a witness in certain respects. Fed. R. Evid. 408. Settlement letters typically will include some indication that the offer is intended to fall within the protections of this rule.

purchase of Parth, which is a key element of the company's costs. As a small business operating three retail locations in the Denver area, Nowecki is constantly monitoring and attempting to control the costs of its operations. Nowecki promptly and reasonably mitigated its damages in this case by arranging a one-year supply contract for Parth with Northern Chemical at $110 per pound effective January 5, 2012.

The sharp increase in the market price for Parth starting in late 2012 did not excuse 3C from its legal obligation to supply Nowecki with Parth at the agreed-upon price for the agreed-upon term of the contract. 3C expressly assumed the risk of such a price increase by agreeing to the three-year fixed-price supply contract. As a result of 3C's breach of that contract beginning on January 1, 2012, Nowecki suffered a loss of $90,000, as determined by the difference between the 3C contract price and the contract price with Northern for the approximately 1,500 pounds of Parth that Nowecki anticipates purchasing in 2012.

Because these facts are undisputed and the material breach of the supply contract is patent, Nowecki will be entitled to summary judgment. In the unlikely event that this case proceeds to trial, a Denver County jury would find a breach of contract and award the simply calculable $90,000 in damages. When considering costs that could be recoverable by Nowecki,[15] my client's settlement offer of $83,000 represents a savings to 3C of approximately 10% over the damages award that will result in this matter. Of course, the foregone litigation expense constitutes a further gain to both parties from settlement.

We appreciate your client's consideration of this offer. This offer, unless withdrawn, will remain available for acceptance by your client until November 7, 2012.

Sincerely,

Woo Jin Park

9.3.2   3C RESPONSIVE OFFER LETTER

October 11, 2012

BY PERSONAL DELIVERY

Confidential and Non-Admissible

Woo Jin Park
Park and Associates
1900 Logan Street #1100
Denver, CO 80203

Re: Nowecki Dry Cleaning, Inc. v. CleanChem Company:

---

[15] Litigation "costs" are distinct from attorney's fees. *See* section 8.1.2.

Court File No. 12–cv–035; Our File No. GC–847390

Dear Mr. Park:

Thank you for your letter dated September 28, 2012. I have spoken with my client, CleanChem Company ("3C"), about your settlement offer. The cost of bringing this case to trial—a result we believe is the likely outcome of continued litigation—would greatly exceed any reasonable chance of recovery by Nowecki Dry Cleaners, Inc. ("Nowecki"). Accordingly, 3C shares your client's interest in efficiently resolving this matter through settlement, if possible.

We do not agree, however, with the position articulated in your letter that this case presents simple legal questions based on uncomplicated facts. I will briefly note two of the issues that will be presented to the court in any dispositive motion briefing.

First, the contract at issue contained a force majeure clause that excused performance for reasons beyond the control of the parties. Specifically, the contract provides that performance is excused as a result of "...acts of God, strikes, accidents, *war*, explosions, floods, or any other cause that is beyond the reasonable control of that party." (Emphasis added). 3C was unable to provide Parth at $50/pound as a consequence of a civil war impacting its supply chain. In *Interpetrol Bermuda Ltd. v. Kaiser Aluminum International Corp.*, 719 F.2d 992 (9th Cir. 1983), the court excused seller performance for reasons of inability to obtain the agreed commodity from its supply chain.

Second, Nowecki rushed into a one-year supply contract within a week of receiving notice from 3C of the supply problems beyond its control. Even if Nowecki is able to prevail on all issues related to liability, it failed to act reasonably in mitigating its damages and thus is not entitled to its demand of $90,000. A plaintiff is not entitled to claimed damages when it fails "to exercise reasonable care and diligence to minimize or lessen damages." *Berger v. Sec. Pac. Info. Sys., Inc.*, 795 P.2d 1380, 1385 (Colo.App. 1990). Nowecki agreed to a supply contract for Parth at the highest possible price point in the market; in fact, at its highest price point in history. The market for this chemical was clearly in turmoil in early January, 2012 and we are prepared to offer expert testimony that entering into a one-year contract in that turbulent market was not reasonable market conduct. This expert testimony will be bolstered by the fact that the market price for Parth has now fallen to $76 per pound—far less than the $110 per pound that Nowecki hastily agreed to pay to one of 3C's competitors at the height of the market.

The above issues are just a few of the legal and factual questions that will need to be resolved by the court or at trial should litigation of this case continue.[16] Given the additional expenses that will be incurred by both parties if such judicial resolution is required, 3C has authorized a $20,000 settlement payment to Nowecki Dry Cleaners, Inc. to resolve the lawsuit.

Attached is a Settlement Agreement providing for the $20,000 payment.[17] The Agreement includes a confidentiality clause, a full release of all claims by Nowecki and other standard settlement terms.[18] A check for $20,000 will be delivered to Nowecki within 48 hours of our receipt of the executed Agreement.

This settlement offer is withdrawn if an executed copy of the Settlement Agreement is not received in our offices by the end of business on October 25, 2012.

Best Wishes,

Cheryl Houghton
Senior Partner
Mickey, Katzen and Tesker, P.A.

---

[16] Nowecki's settlement offer letter presents the case as a near certain win given the blatant nonperformance on the contract by the defendant for the final year of the term. 3C's letter can be seen as aimed directly at Mr. Nowecki. The defendant is trying to unsettle Mr. Nowecki as to the chances of Nowecki Dry Cleaners prevailing in the litigation. If 3C can raise doubts in Mr. Nowecki's mind as to the strength of his company's case, it may be possible to settle the matter for an amount far less than Nowecki's actual damages.

[17] The draft settlement agreement is not reproduced in this text.

[18] It is common for attorneys to reference "standard terms." In some cases, there are standard terms that attorneys within an area of practice incorporated in documents of a given type. In other cases, some items may be common and others less common. Attorneys in this situation will reference "standard terms" as a way to induce opposing counsel, particularly inexperienced opposing counsel, to not look carefully at the proposed settlement terms.

CHAPTER 10

APPEARING BEFORE A JUDGE IN A CHAMBERS CONFERENCE

■ ■ ■

Litigators appear before trial court judges in three distinct settings: trial, motion hearings and informal adjudication. Advocacy by the attorney at motion hearings is either a subject of first year legal writing and advocacy courses, or is similar to appellate argument, which is usually covered in such courses. Trial practice is typically the subject of upper level courses designed for aspiring litigators. This chapter focuses on informal adjudication by courts.

10.1 INTRODUCTION TO CHAMBERS CONFERENCES

A modern chambers conference is an informal meeting of the judges and the attorneys for the parties to discuss matters that arise during the litigation. The chambers conference usually is attended by the opposing attorneys without clients. Court reporters usually are not present, and thus there typically is not an official record of the proceeding.[1]

Chambers conferences can occur at the request of the parties or the court, or can happen as a routine matter in litigation. Chambers conferences are sometimes more administrative in nature. For instance, the pretrial conference required under Rule 16 of the Federal Rules of Civil Procedure typically occurs before a federal magistrate judge in the form of a chambers conference.[2] Judges sometimes schedule periodic chambers conferences in especially complex matters to ensure that the litigation is proceeding properly and expeditiously. Other chambers conferences occur because the parties seek the judge's assistance in resolving a dispute. Such conferences may involve disagreements over discovery (e.g., whether a party should be required to produce certain documents), trial arrangements (e.g., whether certain witnesses will be permitted or the admissibility of exhibits), settlement or other matters.

---

[1] Chambers conferences also happen in criminal matters and some commentators and advocates have questioned whether the failure to create a record in this setting violates the criminal defendant's constitutional rights. Raisa Litmanovich, *In the Name of Efficiency: How the Massachusetts District Courts are Lobbying Away the Constitutional Rights of Indigent Defendants*, 29 B.C. Third World L.J. 293 (2009).

[2] FED. R. CIV. P. 16(b).

Learning to interact with a judge during informal adjudication is critical to becoming a successful litigator because judges shape and share their impression of cases partly through these informal interactions, and because the decisions made as part of informal adjudication can be important to the outcome of the case. Understanding chambers conferences also is a means of understanding how judges think about their jobs. Chambers conferences are more likely to involve rapid give and take and often result in an "on the spot" decision by the judge about how to handle the dispute or resolve the issues that gave rise to the conference.

10.2   PERSUASION IN CHAMBERS CONFERENCE

A chambers conference is neither a negotiation nor a motion hearing, but it often will have elements of both. As in negotiations and motion arguments, attorneys need to employ skills of persuasion when presenting their positions to the court. Success in the chambers conference often will be a matter of effectively presenting a rationale and a narrative in support of a desired outcome.

10.2.1 RATIONALE

Whenever an attorney makes a demand in negotiations or to the court, he should be able to articulate a clear rationale for why the opposing party or court should agree to the demand. In the context of an appellate argument, the attorney ostensibly is arguing a legal rationale. The appellant's attorney is asserting that the lower court made an error of law that requires overturning the outcome ordered by that court.

The rationale in a chambers conference can be more elusive because the attorney often is required to present reasons for the court to take an action over which it has broad discretion under the law. For example, the argument over appointment of a mediator in the Chambers Conference video is not about applying the facts of the case to the law, but rather is about making a decision that almost surely will not be reviewed by an appellate court. The parties have a disagreement and the judge is consulted to help them resolve the matter, which she effectively accomplishes by imposing a deadline for the parties to resolve the matter along with a threatened judicially imposed result in case the parties do not reach agreement. This sort of practical decision-making requires that the attorneys present to the judge a rationale for their position, just not the same type of rationale as occurs in a formalized appellate argument.

Identify the outcome that you want from the Chambers Conference and then finish the following sentence: "The (desired outcome) is appropriate here because…" This is rationale—a reason or reasons that the court should make a decision or assert pressure on one side or the other so as to achieve the attorney's desired objective. For each outcome that you seek at a chambers conference, you should be able to provide a succinct rationale.

10.2.2 FRAMING

The chambers conference usually focuses on narrow issues and concerns related to the procedural and discovery rights of the parties during the course of the litigation. Nonetheless, every appearance before the judge is an opportunity to shape the judge's overall impression of your case. The attorney should have a firm grasp of the narrative of the case and look for appropriate opportunities to present that narrative in the chambers conference.

When the chambers conference involves a matter in dispute between the parties, such as in the upcoming simulation, attorneys also should have a focused narrative that will help persuade the judge why the attorney's preferred outcome is a fair resolution. This narrative can involve, among other things, the relationship of the opposing attorneys or parties in the attempted resolution of the dispute, the consequence of the issue for the broader dispute, the general policy concerns of the court or the court's resource limits.

10.3   MAKING THE MOST OF LIMITED JUDICIAL TIME

Trial court judges are busy and often overwhelmed with work. For example, "[a]n annual study . . . shows Montana judges are overburdened by a workload that sees them handling as many as 85 matters a day and more."[3] The fact that trial court judges are busy means that the attorney has to be succinct in presenting her position to the court, which requires that the attorney knows her priority goals for the conference and knows the case file well.

Know what you want. Chambers conferences usually involve a chance for the attorneys to present their concerns to the court. The attorney needs to be able to articulate precisely his concerns and desired resolution. If there are multiple matters at issue, the attorney should know which matters are higher priority and try to focus the conference on those matters when the opportunity is presented.

Know the case file. At an appellate argument, the attorneys can presume that the judges have read carefully the extensive briefs and know the details of the argument before the court. At a trial court chambers conference, the judge may only know the general outline of the case and

---

[3] The Associated Press, *Study: Montana Judges Work Too Much*, GREAT FALLS TRIB., DEC. 10, 2012, http://www.greatfallstribune.com/viewart/20121209/NEWS01/312090026/Study-Montana-judges-work-too-much-only-two-districts-enough-judges.

of the specific dispute or issue that is before the court. The judge simply does not have the time to know the case as well as the attorneys. The attorney has to know the case file and be able to answer the judge's questions about the details of the litigation.

10.4 NAVIGATING JUDICIAL DIFFERENCE

Predictability is difficult to obtain in endeavors that involve people. Courts are no exception. Every judge you encounter will expect that you act respectfully and professionally, and that you know the details of the matter that is before the court. Yet judges vary substantially in how they interact with attorneys in chambers.

Some judges will be solicitous of the views of the attorneys who appear in their chambers, while other judges are more comfortable fully directing the discussion. Some judges like to make decisions resolving disputes during the conference, while other judges use the conference as a means to help the parties find an agreed solution. Judges also will vary in how strictly they apply the limits in the discovery rules, about their willingness to amend scheduling deadlines, about the time they will devote to a chambers conference, about the formality of their interactions with the attorneys, as well as in a variety of other ways.

Practicing attorneys learn to adapt to different perspectives and styles when appearing in front of trial court judges. It is important for young attorneys to pay attention to what the judge expects in her courtroom and chambers, and to adapt accordingly.

CHAPTER 11

MEDIATION: FACILITATED NEGOTIATION AND CLIENT PREPARATION

■ ■ ■

Parties engaged in disputes frequently use mediation in an attempt to reach a settlement. Mediation occurs voluntarily or by court system directive to engage in some form of alternative dispute resolution (ADR).[1] Litigants and their attorneys often prefer mediation as a means of ADR because it is non-binding and less expensive.

In mediation, a neutral mediator attempts to facilitate settlement but does not possess the authority to order a resolution. In contrast, binding arbitration is an ADR process in which the arbitrator replaces a judge or jury as the decision-maker in the matter. Mediation generally is less expensive than binding ADR mechanisms because it does not require the attorneys to present testimony or other evidence in a trial-like setting.

Section 11.1 begins by explaining the mediation process and the role of the mediator. Section 11.2 examines client counseling prior to mediation for a case involving distributive negotiation. Section 11.3 looks at settlement strategy in mediation. Section 11.4 focuses on sharing or acquiring information during mediation.

11.1 INTRODUCTION TO MEDIATION

Mediation is a meeting rather than a formal decision-making tribunal. Mediation nonetheless has conventions and is to some extent governed by law. The first subsection explicates the people and processes typically involved in mediation. The following subsection discusses the interaction between the attorney and the mediator, and the differing goals of the mediator and the attorney's client.

11.1.1 MEDIATION BASICS

Mediation in litigation typically is attended by the mediator, the parties and the attorneys for the parties, although the composition of the

---

[1] *E.g.*, MICH. CT. R. 2.410. Parties involved in a dispute sometimes attempt to settle the matter through mediation prior to initiating litigation.

mediation will vary with the context of the lawsuit.[2] Mediators usually will require that the parties attend the mediation. In the case of an organizational party, mediators routinely require that the organization send a person with decision-making authority over the litigation.

In a case of any complexity in which the parties are represented by attorneys, each attorney typically will send a confidential brief to the mediator prior to the mediation. This brief will summarize each party's view of the facts and merits of the case, the settlement positions of the party and other information that the party determines will assist the mediator in understanding the dispute from its perspective. Mediators use these briefs and key court filings in the case to gain an understanding of the dispute prior to the mediation.

Mediation usually can be described as a form of shuttle diplomacy. Mediators sometime begin the mediation by having all parties meet together to go over the mediation process and to discuss the value of settlement in litigation, and mediators sometimes bring the parties together at the end of the mediation. Whether or not the mediator pulls the parties together at the beginning or end of the mediation, or never does so, most of the mediation usually involves the mediator directing the parties to separate rooms and meeting with each party individually. These separate meetings are known as "private caucuses."[3]

The mediator goes back and forth between the parties conveying information and settlement offers, and discussing the case and the settlement position with each party. The mediator often will share her view of the merits of the case, including evaluations of the likelihood of success on dispositive motion or at trial.[4] The mediator will share some of the information provided by one party with the other party when she determines that this information will help move the settlement position of the litigants. In most jurisdictions, communication during the mediation process is considered privileged and cannot be disclosed by the litigants, parties, or mediator.[5]

A defining feature of mediation is that the mediator is a neutral third party whose job is to impartially resolve the dispute. Some jurisdictions

---

[2] Some family law mediations, for instance, routinely exclude attorneys from the process. Similarly, an attorney for the borrower usually is not present in mediation required under state law prior to foreclosure by a mortgage lender.

[3] On the other hand, a few mediators will keep the parties together during the entire mediation.

[4] Mediators have different approaches to the process. Some mediators actively evaluate the merits of the case and share this information with the parties. A few mediators in litigated matters take a solely facilitative role and do not offer their views on the merits of the dispute.

[5] Alan Kirtley, *The Mediation Privilege's Transition from Theory to Implementation: Designing a Mediation Privilege Standard to Protect Mediation Participants, the Process and the Public Interest,* 1995 J. DISP. RESOL. 1, 15 (1995).

require that the mediator have specific qualifications or training.[6] As with judges, neutral does not mean inhuman. Mediators come to the process with varying types of expertise, experience and perspectives. Because the mediator may offer her view about the legal and other merits of the case and because that view may have an impact on a party's evaluation of the case, attorneys usually seek out a mediator who knows the law and practice in the area of dispute and who, at the least, will not be empathetic with the opposing party's position. No plaintiff's attorney wants to advise an injured client that he has a very good chance of winning at trial and recovering more than $100,000 only to have a mediator who has spent her entire career representing insurance companies tell the client, "I have done more than 200 jury trials and my opinion is that there is almost no chance of a judgment more than $20,000 even if the jury believes your story."

11.1.2 MEDIATOR GOALS AND CLIENT GOALS

Mediators settle cases. Mediators have different views about the importance of maintaining a positive relationship between the parties during the process and achieving a result consistent with at least a reasonable outcome in adjudication, but almost every mediator considers obtaining a settlement as her primary objective.[7]

Settling a case should not be the purpose of mediation for the litigant, unless the client is in a position where settlement at the mediation is the only acceptable option. Nor is the mediation the last opportunity to settle a case. Settlement at the mediation is a good outcome only if the settlement terms align with the client's analysis of the value of the case and the client's goals for resolving the dispute.

This mismatch in purpose between the mediator and the parties is important to understand when considering how the mediator relates to the attorneys and the parties. Mediators often will push the attorneys and the client to settle. As noted above, in many cases the mediator will pressure the parties to alter their positions by challenging their evaluation of the merits of the case, which is to say the attorneys' evaluation of the case in most instances.[8] The attorney should carefully

---

[6] Paula M. Young, *Take It Or Leave It. Lump It Or Grieve It: Designing Mediator Complaint Systems That Protect Mediators, Unhappy Parties, Attorneys, Courts, the Process, and the Field*, 21 OHIO ST. J. ON DISP. RESOL. 721, 733 n.43 (2006). Mediators are regulated differently among jurisdictions, resulting in varying requirements related to ethics, qualifications, confidentiality, engaging in the practice of law and other matters. *Id.* at 731–41.

[7] *See, e.g.,* Mark K. Schonfield, *Hidden Traps: The Philosophical Considerations in Choosing Mediators and Arbitrators*, 61 OR. ST. B. BULL., Dec. 2000, at 17 (offering a practitioner's view on mediation selection and the goals of mediators).

[8] In some cases, the attorney may be articulating a client position at the mediation with which the attorney disagrees, and thus the attorney will tacitly appreciate the mediator's attack on the client's position. For instance, an attorney may have advised the client that it faces a substantial risk of losing on summary judgment and thus should seek substantially less than its

listen to and evaluate the mediator's criticism. Possible attorney responses include the following:

* *Defend.* If you disagree with the mediator, and the disagreement is of consequence, you can argue your position. You can tell the mediator that she misunderstands the facts or your position, or argue your view of the law, as appropriate. If you convince the mediator that you have properly analyzed the situation, the mediator's reversal of position may help persuade the mediator that you have more properly valued the case. But a mediator is not a judge and your response to the mediator's criticism is not usually solely for the purpose of persuading her. Rather, defending your position communicates to the mediator that your client will not change his or her settlement position based on this concern, if that is the message you intend to convey (and communicates to the client that you are confident in your analysis of the merits of the case).

* *Concede.* Almost any case in mediation during litigation will have a weakness, either in proof or law, or both. It is possible to admit the weaknesses in your case to the mediator if you agree with her evaluation. A concession can be useful for at least three reasons. First, it shows that you have objectively analyzed the case and are in control of the issues in the case. Alternatively, a second reason to concede a point is that you were unaware of information or analysis that genuinely alters your client's settlement position. For example, the mediator may observe an overlooked clause in a contract that could change your view of the merits. Third, a concession can provide a basis for moving your settlement position when you want to do so but need a rationale. *See* Section 11.3.3 below.

A word of caution is in order on the matter of conceding to the mediator adverse facts or law. Make sure you know whether the mediator believes she is authorized to share this concession with the opposing party. *See* Section 11.4 below.

* *Deflect.* Another option is to just acknowledge the criticism and move on to another point. For instance, you can say to the mediator, "I understand your point but don't agree. The real issue here is whether the plaintiff is flexible on the dollar amount." You can later privately advise your client that the mediator is correct or incorrect in your opinion. Ignoring the

---

full loss during the mediation, but the client has rejected this advice and refuses to compromise on its demand for full compensation. The attorney in this situation may welcome the mediator's unfavorable assessment of the legal merits as support for the attorney's efforts to induce client flexibility in settlement position.

issue signals that you do not intend to change your settlement position for that reason without having to engage on the issue.

Regardless of how the attorney responds to the mediator's evaluation of the merits of the case, it is critical that his demeanor be respectful and not excessively argumentative. The mediator is evaluating the attorneys as well as the parties as to a path toward settlement. An attorney who presents as hostile and argumentative can run the risk of having the mediator subtly suggest or even expressly state to the client that the attorney appears to be an obstacle to a reasonable settlement. The attorney's reputation and other factors almost always favor an approach that is civil and cooperative in mediation.[9]

11.2 CLIENT COUNSELING PRIOR TO MEDIATION

The attorney analyzes the merits of the case and the attorney tries to determine the existence or contours of the ZOPA. The client makes the determination of a reservation price and will make the decisions about the initial settlement offer, changes in settlement offers and whether to settle the case or continue the litigation. This section examines effectively presenting the merits to a client when valuing a case that involves distributive negotiations between two parties. This subsection also discusses preparing the client for the mediation process. These critical tasks are part of the larger concern of client counseling. Chapter 14 will re-visit client counseling in more detail and in other situations.

11.2.1 VALUING THE CASE WITH YOUR CLIENT

Put yourself in the position of Mehmet Nowecki, the owner of Nowecki Dry Cleaners. Nowecki has filed a lawsuit against 3C, which has responded with an Answer. The parties have exchanged key documents and agreed that no further discovery is necessary in the case. Nowecki has made an offer to dismiss the litigation in exchange for a payment of $83,000. 3C has responded with an offer of $20,000. Nowecki's attorney

---

[9] Another reason to present to the mediator as reasonable and cooperative is that mediators often report to the judge on the process of the mediation and on the mediator's impression of the conduct and positions of the parties. Parties seen as recalcitrant or unreasonable in settlement may be viewed negatively by the judge. In some cases, the judge or other decision-maker is the mediator. Even when the mediator is outside the judiciary, mediators may talk with judges or personnel in the judge's chambers. Although the law in many jurisdictions would seem to prohibit such communications as a violation of mediation confidentiality, such communications occur. Researchers have established that the mediation confidentiality rule often is breached by attorneys and courts. James R. Coben & Peter R. Thompson, *Disputing Irony: A Systematic Look at Litigation About Mediation*, 11 HARV. NEGOT. L. REV. 43, 48 (2006) (observing that "concerns about confidentiality, paramount among ADR scholars, appear to be of much lesser importance to practitioners, lawyers, and judges in the context of adversarial litigation."); Sara Rudolph Cole, *Protecting Confidentiality in Mediation: A Promise Unfulfilled?*, 54 U. KAN. L. REV. 1419 (2006).

meets Mr. Nowecki before mediation begins in the case and says the following:

> Mehmet, we need to get a good idea of your bottom line before we start the mediation. But first I need to tell you where we are at in the litigation. If we don't settle today, we should move for summary judgment. I think that there is about an 80% chance we will win on dispositive motion, but you never know—it wouldn't be a surprise if we have to go to trial. If we do go to trial, I have to think our chances are very good. But again you never know—it wouldn't surprise me if a jury came back with less than the full $90,000 even if we win, and litigation costs will eat up a lot of that award. So, I would suggest a reservation price here of $65,000, but that is totally up to you. What do you want to do on setting a bottom line?

If you were Mehmet Nowecki, how would you respond to this question? As you read the remainder of this section, consider how Mr. Nowecki's attorney could have interacted with him in a way that increased Mr. Nowecki's confidence about his decision on a reservation price and built better trust in their long-term relationship.

One of the most difficult tasks facing an attorney in some cases is counseling the client regarding a reservation price for mediation. Clients have expectations and hopes that are unlikely to be met in a negotiated settlement with an opposing party who may have the opposite expectations and hopes. This section discusses the process of working with the client to arrive at a reservation price that is consistent with the client's goals, that is a number that the client understands and "owns" as her own choice, and that is presented in a way that will further the trust relationship whether or not the case settles during the impending mediation.

Plain Meaning. The client has to understand the litigation process to understand the risks and possible rewards in litigation. The attorney may not consider that terms familiar to him, like "summary judgment," may not be known or fully understood by the client. And it can be tempting for an attorney, especially a new attorney, to bedazzle the client with a show of expertise by using the language of civil procedure and legal doctrine to describe the litigation situation. Resist that temptation.

Conveying the meaning of the litigation process requires clear communication in two respects. First, use plain language whenever possible in client counseling. Instead of discussing with a defendant client the "probability of prevailing on all claims with our dispositive motion," discuss "the chance that the judge might decide the case for us so that we won't ever see the jury." Legal claims can involve technical terms that are not known by most people. Few small business clients will know what the attorney means by "X is a condition precedent to your claim of contract breach." Everyone will understand when an attorney says, "We have to prove X before we have a chance of winning on your claim that Smith broke the contract."

Second, accurately conveying to the client the litigation situation he faces requires explaining the sequence and consequences of events in the litigation. For example, it is easy to forget that the client may not know what discovery entails, when it will occur in the litigation, how much it will cost, the disruption for the client, and the consequence if the client fails to properly request or produce information in discovery. The attorney needs to explain as much of the litigation process as the client needs to know to make a fully informed judgment about settlement.

The language and detail used to describe the client's litigation situation will vary with the sophistication of the client. A longshoreman who never finished high school who is trying to recover money from a heavy equipment manufacturer for crippling disabilities likely needs a lot of education in plain terms about what might happen in the lawsuit. The opposing attorney representing the manufacturer whose client has been involved in numerous such lawsuits has a very different task. Gauge the knowledge of the client and use language that is appropriate for that person.

Managing Client Expectations. The same well-tested and enduring psychological principle of "anchors" that shapes initial settlement offers can work to shape client expectations in setting a reservation price. A statement by the attorney about the amount of likely recovery or adverse judgment can become embedded in the client's mind as the anchor against which settlement and success in the litigation is judged. Professor Marjorie Corman Aaron, who is an active mediator and arbitrator, warns attorneys as follows about providing the client with specific numbers at the outset of the litigation:

> AVOID creating client expectations and PARTICULARLY avoid mentioning numbers at the outset. No matter how many times you say "only if," "assuming everything breaks our way," or "in the best case scenario," your client will remember the number and forget the caveats and contingencies. Despite your outstanding representation in a difficult case, the client is more likely to feel disappointed.[10]

Yet by the time the client faces mediation, it is not possible to discuss arriving at a reservation price without discussing some specific numbers. The three concerns presented below (client involvement, client decision-making, and percentages versus descriptors) address this central problem

---

[10] MARJORIE CORMAN AARON, CLIENT SCIENCE: ADVICE FOR LAWYERS ON COUNSELING CLIENTS THROUGH BAD NEWS AND OTHER LEGAL REALITIES 169 (2012) (emphasis in original).

raised by Professor Aaron about managing client expectations in settling litigation.

Client Involvement.   One way the attorney can create realistic expectations for the client and achieve a better result in valuing the case with the client is by involving the client in a careful review of the client's position in the litigation. Start by inquiring of the client whether he has any new information about the matter or has any questions or concerns since the last time the attorney talked with the client. This inquiry not only can elicit useful information from the client, it also signals to the client that the attorney is listening carefully to the client's needs and seeking the client's involvement in the evaluative process.

Then, break down each impending or possible step in the litigation and involve the client in the analysis. At each step, explain the situation the attorney and the client will face and invite the client to share information, express concerns or ask questions. For instance, Mr. Nowecki's attorney might have summarized the litigation process as follows:

> Mehmet, let's start by looking at what we face in this case if we don't reach a settlement today. First, we will want to ask the court to decide the case. That process is called "summary judgment," and it will take about 2 to 6 months by the time we get a judge's ruling. If we don't win with the summary judgment approach, the next step will either be to go before a jury or re- start settlement discussions. We probably won't see a jury until about a year from today if we decide to go with a jury. Let's start by talking about our chances on the summary judgment motion before the judge. But before we do that, do you have any questions about how the litigation process works?

After answering any questions, Nowecki's attorney then can begin to describe the probable outcome of a summary judgment motion, the likely result if the judge orders summary judgment, how much it will cost in legal fees and other considerations of consequence to the client. Following the discussion of summary judgment, the attorney can proceed to describe the settlement environment if Nowecki does not prevail on the motion (less favorable than today) and the costs, chance of prevailing, and possible award if Nowecki must take the case to trial.

Client Decision-Making.   The client, of course, makes the ultimate decision on a reservation price. The attorney's job is to engage with the client on a range of possible specific outcomes in the litigation while leading the client to take responsibility for and ownership over the final decision. Consider the difference between these two presentations of the same case by a defense attorney to her client.

Attorney A: Harriet, let's review what we have discussed. We
have two chances for winning this case outright. We have as
good a chance of winning the motion before the judge as we do of
losing it, and if we win that motion the case may be over,
depending on what the judge decides. If we don't win that
motion, we will have to go to trial. We have talked a lot about
that. I like our chances before the judge better than our chances
before a jury. If we have to go to trial AND we lose, then you
will have to factor in our discussion about the amount the jury
could award to Schmidt. The best case is probably about
$100,000, but as we discussed, that is not very likely. Equally
unlikely, but still possible, is an award of up to $500,000. Your
litigation costs also will be about $35,000 more if we have to go
to trial. So what are your initial questions or thoughts about a
top number to have in mind as we go into mediation?

Attorney B: Harriet, let's review what we have discussed. We
have two chances for winning this case outright. The first is if
the judge orders that Schmidt's case be dismissed entirely. I
give us a 50/50 chance on that outcome. If we have to go trial, I
think our chances of winning are less—say, about 25%. If we lose
at trial, I think Schmidt will be awarded somewhere between
$100,000 and $500,000. I would give us at least a 50% chance of
keeping such an award under $250,000. And don't forget that
our legal costs will top $35,000 if we go to trial. If you total up
all of this, a top number for settlement in the neighborhood of
$100,000 or a little more would be reasonable at this point. But
I know you have a lot to consider here. What do you think makes
sense for setting as our top number to have in mind as we go into
mediation?

A key difference in these two scenarios is that the first attorney ended the
summary of the case merits and costs by engaging the client in deriving a
reservation price.   The second attorney suggested a number for
reservation price based on the analysis presented by the attorney. Both
approaches are proper, but there are three important reasons for taking
the first approach in most cases.

First, forcing the client to grapple with all the information and come up
with a reservation price often can lead to better decision-making. The
client usually is in the best position to mesh the risks of litigation with
the client's articulated and unarticulated non-monetary concerns and risk
tolerance. Even an attorney who has carefully gauged what the client has
said about non-monetary concerns and risk tolerance cannot substitute
for the client's own judgment about these concerns in processing the
litigation risks presented by the attorney. Furthermore, when the client
is faced with the choice of making counter-offers in settlement, having

been fully involved in and taking control of the reservation price setting process will place the client in a better position to make decisions consistent with an effective negotiating strategy.

Second, the client who derives a reservation price herself rather than accedes to or adjusts the number provided by the attorney "owns" the number. This helps avoid the problem articulated by Professor Aaron where the attorney does outstanding work, but the client judges the attorney by the psychological anchor presented early in the case as a "best outcome." It also avoids the related problem of the attorney suggesting a number more easily reached as a way of lowering client expectations.

Third, client decision-making as to the derivation of reservation price helps the client accept bad news. A common difficulty in setting a reservation price with the client is that the attorney's analysis of the case is moving beyond the client's ideals and introducing the client, maybe for the first time in a comprehensive way, to the reality of how others might see the case. The attorney helping the client value the case is forcing the client to accept that he may not or even probably will not receive (or pay) anything close to his initial expectations. Having the client make the decision as to a reservation price after hearing about the risks in litigation can help the client internalize the reality that settlement will dash his initial hopes in the litigation.

None of this means that the attorney shouldn't have a clear idea of her views on the value of the case before meeting with the client. It is important for the attorney to estimate objectively the value of the case before talking with the client. The attorney will be in command of all the information needed to set a reservation price only if the attorney has already completed that analysis herself. And the attorney with a case value in mind will be in a better position to understand how the client is thinking about the problem of deriving reservation price, and thus will be able to ask the client questions or provide direction when the client's decisions do not seem clear-headed and rational.[11]

For instance, if Mr. Nowecki listens to the attorney's description of the litigation risks and then says, "I am really worried about whether 3C will even be around to pay if we win with the judge or the jury, and I really need the money now or I may not be able to stay in business, so let's not take a penny less than $80,000 in this mediation," his articulation of non-monetary concerns strongly suggesting settlement and risk avoidance do not seem to square with his setting a reservation price almost as high as Nowecki could expect to obtain in litigation. The attorney can recognize

---

[11] A complete discussion of advising clients who make apparently irrational decision is beyond the scope of this text. For a useful discussion of this task, *see* DAVID A. BINDER, ET AL., LAWYERS AS COUNSELORS: A CLIENT CENTERED APPROACH 429–40 (3d ed. 2012).

and understand this problem if the attorney has already derived her view of the merits as to settlement price.

What if the client says: "I just want to know what you think we should set as our bottom line. I trust your judgment."? The attorney can deflect the question, answer from the perspective of the client as her goals and concerns have been articulated, or answer as to what the attorney would do if she were the client. There is no correct answer. Just be prepared for the question and know which of these choices you would select and why you would answer in that way.[12]

Percentages versus Descriptors. Another difference between the two scenarios above is that attorney B used percentages to indicate the chance of success at each stage of the proceedings, while attorney A used descriptive words. The question of whether to use percentages or descriptors is a more specific concern than the general concepts discussed above, but it is an omnipresent issue in communicating with a client about reservation price, so it is worth some thought. Each approach has its advantages.

Percentages provide the client with a short-hand means to more clearly understand the attorney's evaluation of litigation risk. Percentages convey precision, even when the attorney uses qualifying language. Attorney A says, "I like our chances before the judge better than our chances before a jury," while Attorney B offers the specific evaluation of a 25% chance the jury will find for the defendant-client versus a 50% chance of success with the motion before the judge. The percentage estimate offers a rational client a clear means of evaluating risk: if the defendant is forced to go to trial, the expected cost of the verdict is .75 (the chance of the plaintiff prevailing before the jury) multiplied by the expected amount of a verdict against the defendant. This type of numerical analysis offers a simple and precise means of weighing the litigation risk of trial.[13]

The downside of offering percentage estimates of success in litigation is that their precision can be illusory and can present the same problems as giving the client advice as to a specific reservation price. Percentages are no more than a short-hand employed by the attorney to assist in explaining outcome risks. Every component factored into determining that number, no more how rigorous and detailed the thought process, involves guesswork and judgment. But clients often take percentages literally and seriously. Disclaimers that the percentage is just a numerical expression of a guess may be forgotten when the litigation is

---

[12] For a discussion of dealing with a direct client question as to settlement position, *see* STEFAN H. KRIEGER & RICHARD K. NEUMANN, JR., ESSENTIAL LAWYERING SKILLS: INTERVIEWING, COUNSELING, NEGOTIATION, AND PERSUASIVE FACT ANALYSIS 278–80 (4th ed. 2011).

[13] Percentage estimates of success are required for each stage of the litigation process if the client wants to use a decision tree to derive the value of the case in litigation. *See* Section 8.1.1.

over and the client just remembers putting pen to paper to make decisions based on the attorney's advice.

Communicating risks in percentages also can amount to the same thing as providing the client with a proposed reservation price. Even if Attorney B ended the conversation with a question that invited the client to talk about a reservation price rather than a proposed number, a client with a calculator and a rudimentary understanding of odds could quickly determine the attorney's estimated value for the litigation. A 50% chance on losing the motion times a 75% chance of losing at trial times a $250,000 mid-point of an anticipated verdict, along with $35,000 in extra litigation costs for trial, is a little more than $100,000 (.50 * .75 * (250,000 + 35,000) = $106,875).

The alternative to this faux precision is to use more general descriptors, as was employed by Attorney A. Examples of such descriptions are "not very likely," "a reasonably good chance of prevailing" and "substantial risk of losing." Some clients may find these vague evaluations evasive or confusing, yet attorneys tend to use them frequently. Descriptors avoid the problems of false precision or specific advice as to a reservation price. There are many attorneys who subscribe to the rule that they will never give the client a precise percentage estimate of litigation risks. An approach favored by other attorneys is to offer descriptors to the client but to be prepared with percentage estimates if the client requests a more precise evaluation.

11.2.2 PREPARATION FOR THE MEDIATION PROCESS

Clients properly prepared for mediation are in control. Control means the client being able to anticipate what might occur so there are as few surprises as possible. A client who has not been properly informed or consulted can react badly either in front of an adverse party or in the presence of a mediator or judge, and this weakens the case. Similarly, a client who knows how and when to participate can leave an impression that creates leverage.

Before engaging in mediation, the attorney should explain to the client the likely process for the mediation. The client must understand that the mediation is a non-binding, facilitated negotiation of the dispute. The attorney should explain that the mediation likely will include private caucuses, and that the mediator likely will shuttle back and forth with offers and information from each side. The client should be told that information shared with the mediator may or may not be shared with the other side, and that the attorney will work with the client during the mediation to ensure that the client understands when information will or will not be shared. The client also should understand that the mediator has already received information about the dispute, including each side's submission of a mediation brief, if that occurred.

It is especially important for the attorney to explain to the client the role of the mediator. A mediator can exert a lot of pressure on the parties. The client should understand that the objective of the mediator is to form an agreement between the parties. Specifically, the attorney should prepare the client to hear adverse and even negative comments about the client's position and chances of prevailing in the matter. If the client is unaware of the mediator's role, the client may mistake the mediator's criticism as a balanced and decisive evaluation of the case, rather than the mediator working both sides to create an environment conducive to settlement.

Finally, the client should be aware of and participate in formulating the strategic plan for the mediation. The following section includes a discussion of client counseling about the anticipated and actual process of making counter-offers in the mediation.

11.3 SETTLEMENT STRATEGY IN MEDIATION

Section 8.3 introduced some basic concepts related to bargaining tactics. This section looks more closely at the process of making offers and counter-offers in negotiating during a two-party mediation that occurs during litigation, and how to develop a plan for that process. Chapter 13 examines negotiating in a multi-dimensional environment.[14]

11.3.1 CONCESSION PATTERNS

Negotiation would be a simple task if the attorney knew the other party's reservation price. The attorney and client could decide if that price was more favorable than the client's reservation price. If so, the client could settle at that price, which is the best offer she could get in the negotiation. If not, the attorney would continue with the litigation. But absent ill-advised trickery, a blunder by the opposing party or great luck, the attorney will not know the opposing party's reservation price.

Instead, most negotiations proceed through a process of making concessions in a series of counter-offers that can be seen as signaling the parties' negotiating position to the other side. The counter-offer amount will be compared to the anchor amounts of the initial offers of the parties and compared to prior concessions by each party.

---

[14] Game theory is one tool for modeling conflict by assuming certain negotiation components (rational players, moves, payoffs, strategies, and rules) as an aid to clarifying negotiating alternatives that are available to a negotiator and an opponent. Game theory scholarship in legal negotiations has tended to focus on one particular tool—the use of the "prisoner's dilemma" game as a means of describing collective action problems. Richard H. McAdams, *Beyond the Prisoner's Dilemma: Coordination Game Theory and Law*, 89 SO. CALIF. L. REV. 209 (2009).

Signals in Concessions. One way to think about the counter-offer process is that each offer is saying something about the offeror's reservation price and its evaluation of the existence and range of ZOPA, in the negotiation. The attorney's job is to evaluate the signals sent from the other side and carefully consider the impact of the signals the client intends to send in making counter-offers.

Return to the Nowecki example. Assume that the situation is pretty much as we left it previously—the reservation prices are $55,000 for Nowecki and $70,000 for 3C; Nowecki made an initial offer of $83,000 and 3C responded with an offer of $20,000. This circumstance can be graphed as follows:

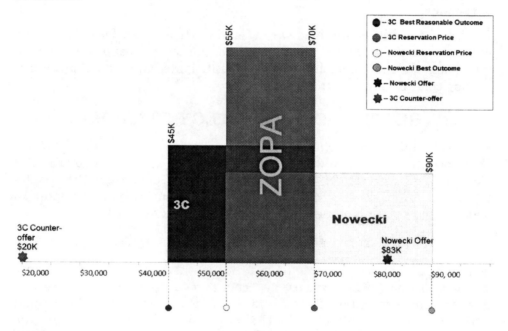

Figure 11–1.

But the above graph is not how the situation appears to each attorney and party. Consider the situation from Nowecki's perspective. All Nowecki knows for sure is its own reservation price and 3C's offer amount. A chart of known, certain information from Nowecki's perspective looks something like this:

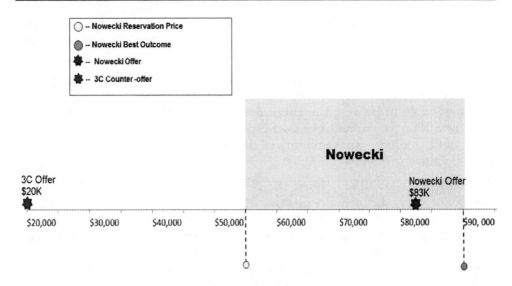

Figure 11–2.

Nowecki's attorney has the task of trying to guess what 3C's side of the chart looks like, and hence whether there is a ZOPA, and if so, the shape of the ZOPA. Nowecki has to gauge the meaning of the $20,000 counter-offer for this purpose. Remember the importance of anchor amounts with initial offers. These initial offers often exert influence in the negotiations and there is a tendency to gravitate toward settlements near the mid-point of the offers. A $20,000 response to an initial offer of $83,000 leaves a "split the difference" amount of $51,500, which is close to but less than Nowecki's reservation price.

Nowecki has to consider whether 3C is signaling that its reservation price is near $51,500 because it values the case at much less than Nowecki, or whether 3C is just attempting to set a low anchor to influence negotiations in its direction. Some knowledge of 3C and its attorneys may help with this evaluation.

Nowecki's attorney has to lay out options for the client"s response. Refusing to counter-offer would signal in the clearest terms that an offer near $51,000 is not close to acceptable to Nowecki, suggesting that Nowecki's reservation price is actually higher than $55,000. Such an offer likely would terminate negotiations, as continued negotiations will occur only if 3C bids against itself or Nowecki retracts its refusal to counter-offer. A substantial concession at this point, reducing its demand to $70,000 for instance, would send the opposite message to 3C—that a settlement near $51,500 is very possible. A $70,000 offer likely will mean Nowecki can settle for its reservation price of $55,000 if 3C matches Nowecki's concession. Between these poles, lies a sliding scale of negligible counter-offers suggesting some willingness to keep talking yet little confidence that a ZOPA exists versus generous counter-offers that encourage 3C to think that negotiations are leading to a settlement closer to its preferred outcome.

Counseling the Client on Negotiating Concessions. The attorney will continue to counsel the client as the mediation continues. So what is the attorney's role in helping the client decide on whether to make a counter-offer, and if so, the amount of that counter-offer? This form of counseling often will include an element of interpretation and an element of dispassionate resolve.

The attorney should be helping the client understand the meaning of the concessions by the other side and the signals that would be sent by possible counter-offers from the client. The attorney can help the client interpret the offers and information provided by the other side as signals about what is possible or likely to expect from the end result of the negotiation including the possibility of this concession pattern ending in agreement., In other words, the attorney can help the client by explaining the likely meaning of the evolving concession pattern.

The attorney also can assist the client by serving in the role of objective observer and historian. The client and the attorney have worked together to determine a reservation price prior to the start of the mediation. The attorney can remind a client who is considering moving unfavorably beyond its reservation price of the reason that the attorney and client worked on developing this price—that the client determined there was more value in continued litigation than settling for less (or more) than reservation price. And the attorney can remind the client of its goals in the litigation and use those goals to weigh the value of a settlement versus the value of continued litigation. It can be difficult to learn how to separate this role of detached counselor from the role of advocate that also is part of the mediation process.

Beyond the First Offers. As the negotiating process moves beyond the first responsive counter-offers from each side, the relative movement of the parties compared to past offers assumes importance. Professor Raifa has observed that "the most common pattern" for concessions as negotiations proceed is "monotone decreasing," which he describes as intervals between decreasing offers become successively smaller, which signals the party is approaching its limit."[15] Concessions usually become more grudging as negotiations continue.

Assume that Nowecki and its attorney analyze the situation and determine that 3C's $20,000 initial offer is insufficient to herald promising negotiations. Mehmet Nowecki decides his company would take a chance on obtaining a judgment for its full loss on summary

---

[15] HOWARD RAIFFA, THE ART AND SCIENCE OF NEGOTIATION 128 (1982).

judgment rather than settle in the low end of a possible ZOPA at this time. Nowecki counter-offers with a $1,000 reduction to $82,000. Nowecki's first offer was a $7,000 drop from its demand for full compensation. By making a comparably much smaller concession in the next round, Nowecki has announced that it does not take the $20,000 offer from 3C as a legitimate anchor in the negotiation, although it is not willing to just end negotiations without some responsive offer. 3C now faces the tough choice of sticking with its low offer, thus effectively terminating this round of negotiation, or making a substantial move that signals interest in reaching a negotiated settlement at an amount higher than the $50,000 range.

It is common in mediations for the mediator to ask both parties to "split the difference" once the parties' offer amounts are close enough that it is apparent a settlement is imminent. If the parties in the Norwecki case have completed a sequence of multiple counter-offers that leaves 3C at $58,000 and Nowecki at $64,000, for example, with the last offer seeing only a movement of $1,000 on each side, the mediator likely will attempt to obtain swift agreement on a $61,000 settlement. Few parties want to leave the mediation knowing that they caused the litigation to continue over the last $3,000 to be compromised. And no party wants the judge in the case to hear the same.

Reservation Price and Negotiation Success. This last example raises an important point about the meaning of reservation price in settlement. Reservation price is a settlement amount determined pre-mediation at which continued litigation would be a preferable option. It provides a bright line that the party should not cross in the mediation unless new information changes the party's evaluation of the merits and risks of litigation. That does not mean that a party should settle for its reservation price when that amount is offered by the other side in a given mediation because the goal of the mediation is not to obtain a minimally acceptable settlement, but rather to obtain the best possible settlement under the circumstances.

Think about reservation price as operating differently depending on which direction the mediation is forcing the party to consider moving its settlement offer, as depicted below:

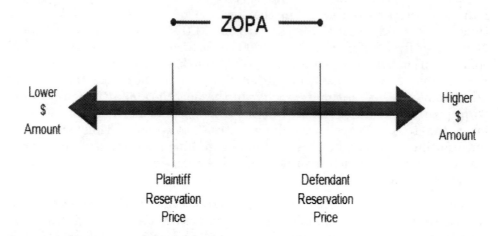

Figure 11–3.

The defendant knows that it would rather litigate than settle for an amount in the blue zone, while the plaintiff knows that it would rather keep litigating than settle for an amount in the red zone. But once the opposing party's offer is in the purple zone, it is nonetheless reasonable to decide to continue pushing for, and even end the mediation for failure to obtain, a result that is a more pleasing shade of purple. Obtaining a reservation price is a necessary, but not sufficient, condition for a party to accept settlement.

11.3.2 PLANNING OFFERS AND CONCESSIONS PRIOR TO MEDIATION

One aspect of offer and concession planning that is solely in the control of each party is their initial position in the mediation. Each party knows the last settlement offer, if any, made prior to the mediation. Now each party has to confront a threshold question—is the party willing to "go first" with an initial offer or concession in the mediation? If the parties have yet to make an offer, each party has to evaluate the relative advantages of making the first offer or resisting making an initial offer.[16] In the mediation simulation, an offer has been made and response received. In this situation, the parties can and should plan whether to make an initial concession in the mediation, and if so, the amount or terms for that concession.

---

[16] Business School Professors Margaret Neale of Stanford and Adam Galinsky of Harvard both argue that the conventional wisdom of waiting for the other party to make an offer is bad advice because of the benefits of the "anchoring" effect discussed in chapter 9. Margaret Neale, *It's Often Smart to Make the First Move in a Negotiation*, at http://www.gsb.stanford.edu/news/headlines/2007nealefirstmove.html; Adam Galinsky, *When to Make First Offers in Negotiation*, at http://hbswk.hbs.edu/archive/4302.html.

Consider using role-play in which the attorney presents the positions expected to be taken by the opposing party and then the attorney and client work together to make responsive offers. If time permits, the attorney can consider varying the scenario with different offer and concession strategies by the opposing party. This process is unlikely to replicate the exact sequence of events that will unfold in the mediation. Instead, planning an offer and concession strategy for the mediation can accomplish more modest objectives, such as helping the client and the attorney determine the client's actual risk profile, allowing the client to understand the consequence of a pattern of offers, and exposing the client to the pressures likely to be placed on him or her during the mediation.

11.3.3 COMMUNICATING COUNTER–OFFERS

The above discussion presents the concession process as if the merits of the case are irrelevant. The language used in communicating counter-offers also is important in the negotiating process.

Finding a rationale for concessions can help with disciplined decision-making and with effectively communicating offers. Rather than just authorizing the mediator to make an offer of $X higher (or lower) than your previous offer, articulate a reason for the concession that justifies the movement in position. Reasons that are not directly related to the merits of the case often will be most persuasive, such as the desire to obtain payment more quickly than possible through litigation, the costs of litigation, or an interest in avoiding publicity. Mediators sometimes raise these types of concerns as a way of providing the parties a rationale for concessions.[17]

In any case, attorneys should communicate offers in a way that indicates its reservation price is not more favorable to the other side's position than previously communicated. In addition to articulating a rationale for the move, some other techniques that can lessen the impact of the concession on the other side's evaluation of the bargaining goals of the party are as follows:

> * *Conditions.* Make clear that the monetary concession is linked to a non-monetary condition. Example: "We are willing to increase our offer to $235,000, but only if Dawson agrees to a blanket confidentiality provisions as to the terms of the settlement and facts underlying the dispute." Conversely, concede on money while at the same time stating certain non-monetary topics are not negotiable, or vice versa. Example: "We

---

[17] In some cases, the rationale will reflect a legitimate concern of the party making the concession. In other cases, the party may use a rationale that does not reflect the real thinking of the party; for example, a rationale that is a legitimate concern of the party but has already been used to effectively discount a prior offer. Be careful not to offer rationales so patently or transparently disingenuous that it harms your credibility as a negotiator.

are increasing our offer to $235,000, but we want to make clear that there we cannot accept a settlement agreement that constrains Dawson's future employment prospects."

* *Request Commensurate Counter-offer.* In addition to cushioning the impact of a concession by offering rationale and explanation, the party can accompany the concession with a request for a similar concession by the opposing party. Example: "We agree that litigation costs may be even higher than we were anticipating, and so we are increasing our offer to $235,000. But the same is true for Dawson and so we would expect a comparable movement on his side."

 * *Warnings and Disclaimers.*   Expressly disclaim that the offer is based on the reasoning of the other side, or warn the other side that you are becoming constrained in your ability to continue negotiating. Examples: "We don't agree that the threat of a further motion to compel discovery justifies any reduction in our monetary demand. We don't see any realistic chance of the judge ordering further discovery at this point in the litigation. We are willing to drop our demand to $350,000, but we are at the point in this process where it is difficult to see how we can move lower than that offer."

* *Speed.* Pay attention to the length of time it takes to make an offer. In some circumstances, a rapid move to concession will signal a lack of confidence in position or willingness to concede more.

11.4   MANAGING INFORMATION IN MEDIATION

The attorney should view the mediation as one step in the course of the litigation. In some cases, the parties may engage in multiple mediations or the parties may continue negotiations without third party facilitation after the mediation, so the initial mediation is just part of an extended negotiation process. If the case does not settle, the attorney can emerge from the mediation in a better or worse position depending on how she handles the flow of information during the mediation process. If the case settles, mediation will be the end point of the litigation.[18]

Attorneys need to manage information in both directions—learning from the opponent and disclosing information to the opponent.   Useful information is more than just reading signals about reservation price and

---

[18] Mediations sometimes result in what appears to be a settlement but the parties are not able to reduce the purported agreement to writing during the mediation and the agreement falls apart in the days following the mediation. This scenario is rather common and generates a substantial amount of litigation over whether the agreement seemingly reached at the mediation is enforceable. Coben & Thompson, *supra* note 9, at 73–89 (reviewing over 568 cases in which a party to mediation later attempted to enforce an alleged settlement).

willingness to settle that will influence the mediation position of the parties. Mediation offers the opportunity to learn about the opposition's strategy, framing, risk profile, interest in settlement, legal theories and facts. Let the mediator share as much information as possible about the other side. If the mediator states that the other side refuses to negotiate on a certain issue, the attorney can consider asking the mediator for the other side's rationale for not negotiating on that issue. Attorneys can pay attention to information that signals the opposing party's view of the case, including the narrative that party presents to the mediator and any specific facts that party reveals or emphasizes.

The converse concern is revealing information and positions during the mediation. Articulating a rationale for settlement positions and an analysis of the case is an essential part of negotiation. But attorneys need to be aware of the consequence in doing so and measure when information sharing is most productive. Facts, client goals and other information possessed by the attorney can be helpful to share in support of reasons for settlement, but this information also may be useful to the other side in continued litigation if the case does not settle.

A starting point in considering when to share information with the mediator is knowing whether the mediator will share with the opposing party the information provided during a private caucus. Some mediators will make clear at the outset of the process that any information provided during the private caucuses will be shared with the side unless the party providing the information makes clear that it is not to be shared. Other mediators articulate the opposite presumption—that all information is not to be shared unless the mediator obtains authorization to do so. Other mediators will not expressly state a principle for when information will be shared, but will handle disclosure on an issue by issue basis. The attorney must track when information disclosed might be shared with the opposing party.

It is possible to share information with the mediator and ask that the information not be shared with the other side. This tactic can be useful especially when it explains what would otherwise appear to be irrational behavior on the part of the attorney or client. Mediators often appreciate receiving information that explains motives because it allows the mediator to evaluate whether settlement is likely or devise possible alternatives that meet one party's concerns that cannot be shared with the other side.

The decision to share adverse information perhaps not known by the opposing party requires balancing the leverage gained during the mediation with possible consequences in continued litigation. The attorney should be aware when information sharing is helpful, on balance, and when this calculus cautions keeping information private.

For example, an attorney may have discovered that a key witness that the other side is telling the mediator will provide critical testimony is planning to move to Europe in the near future. It would rarely make sense to share this information as a means of gaining leverage, as it would alert the opposing party to the possibility of promptly taking a deposition in lieu of trial testimony.

CHAPTER 12

INTRODUCTION TO TRANSACTIONAL LAW

■ ■ ■

Clients employ transactional attorneys in business planning matters, to help construct or formalize deals, and to assist with regulatory compliance. These attorneys outnumber litigators,[1] although this reality is not reflected in television shows about attorneys or even most introductory law school courses. This chapter describes the work and culture of transactional attorneys.

Section 12.1 provides an overview of the services provided by transactional attorneys. Section 12.2 contrasts the work process of transactional attorneys with that of litigators, including the starting point, analytical process and product typical of transactional matters. Finally, section 12.3 discusses the reason transactional attorneys are more likely to emphasize certain work style characteristics in their practice.

12.1 THE REALM OF THE TRANSACTIONAL ATTORNEY

As noted in chapter 1, attorneys often describe law as a bifurcated profession—over here, the litigators; over there, the transactional attorneys. Some specialty fields of law divide neatly between the litigators and the transactional attorneys. In tax law, for instance, attorneys think of themselves as either a tax advisor who helps to structure deals and plan tax-saving strategies, or as a tax litigator who represents clients in disputes with the Internal Revenue Service or other taxing authorities.

Within the rubric of "transactional attorney" are two different functions, sometimes distinct and sometimes interrelated. "Deal Attorneys" help clients structure, negotiate and close transactions. Constructing deals means that there is an opposite party or parties in the transaction. Deal attorneys, therefore, usually work with an opposing counsel or opposing party in negotiating the terms of the transaction.

---

[1] DAVID HOWARTH, LAW AS ENGINEERING: THINKING ABOUT WHAT LAWYERS 23–27 (2013) (compiling data showing that most attorneys are engaged in transactional matters rather than litigation in the United States, England and France).

"Planning/Compliance Attorneys," on the other hand, advise clients in how to structure their personal or business affairs. This type of transactional attorney does not typically deal with an opposing counsel or party, but rather represents clients who want to comply with the law governing their business or conduct or want help managing legal risks or opportunities in structuring their business or conduct. These attorneys often are asked to provide opinions about the legal consequence or permissibility of an action the client wants to take, or to provide advice about options the client is considering.

Transactional attorneys in private practice often work with government officials who promulgate or interpret regulations. Private antitrust attorneys responsible for seeking approval of possible mergers, for example, often work with the divisions of the U. S. Department of Justice, U. S. Federal Trade Commission and state attorneys general offices with authority over mergers and anti-competitive market conduct. Conversely, many public agencies employ attorneys whose work is primarily in planning and compliance, and these attorneys often relate to private counsel who want the agency to make decisions favorable to their clients. For instance, counsel for the United States Consumer Products Safety Commission usually will consult with or receive input from manufacturers and advocacy groups when drafting regulations that govern the content of products that can be sold in U. S. consumer markets.

Transactional attorneys are more likely to represent businesses or other organizations rather than individuals, but both types of clients employ transactional attorneys.[2] Below is a chart showing examples of practice by transactional attorneys.

---

[2] John P. Heinz, et. al., *The Changing Character of Lawyer's Work: Chicago in 1975 and 1995*, 32 Law & Soc'y Rev. 751 (1998). Heinz and his research partners have conceptualized the practice of law as containing two distinct cultures separated by whether the attorney's clients are individuals versus corporations or other organizations.

	Business/Organization Client	Individual Client
Deal Attorney	**Mergers and Acquisitions** – Represents businesses in sale or merger of companies.	**Employment** – Represents individuals negotiating with a prospective or existing employer.
	Commercial Real Estate – Represents entities in sale or lease of commercial buildings or space.	**Residential Real Estate** – Represents people constructing, buying or selling a home.
Planning/ Compliance Attorney	**Corporate** – Identifies and creates form of business enterprise and advises as to proper governance of the enterprise.	**Estate Planning** – Drafts wills, trusts, and estate plans for individuals.
	Data Privacy/ Management – Advises government agencies or businesses in complying with information disclosure and data privacy regulations.	**Immigration** – Assists individuals in obtaining work or residency permits or citizenship status from a national government.

Figure 12–1.

These categories as well as the divide between litigation and transactional work are not rigid classifications. A real estate attorney may specialize in commercial deals and refer clients in disputes or with residential real estate matters to a firm partner or an attorney outside the firm. Conversely, some real estate attorneys will be comfortable handling both commercial and residential transactions, and also will represent clients in litigation when deals "go bad." Nor do these categories effectively describe all forms of legal practice. For example, an attorney advising a public agency about whether to approve a reimbursement request by a contractor likely to dispute a negative decision is not a situation captured well by the distinction between litigation and transactional work.

It is useful, however, to think about these various divisions within legal practice when considering the context of representation, and the type of legal practice that best fits your talents and personality. These categories of legal practice provide a short-hand description of the work of most attorneys. The remainder of this chapter looks at how transactional attorneys practice in contrast to litigators.

12.2   THE WORK OF THE TRANSACTIONAL ATTORNEY

Both litigators and transactional attorneys face the same basic problem. Attorneys start with a base of legal knowledge and attempt to translate the situation presented by clients into language and principles cognizable in law. Yet this translation process occurs differently in litigation and transactional matters.

Litigators typically begin by searching for facts about something that has already occurred, sorting those facts into possible legal claims and then conducting legal research and fact development in an iterative manner. This process leads to an evaluation by the attorney of the merits of those claims. The merits evaluation shapes the advice of the attorney to the client as to the best course of action to take in resolving the client's dispute. The representation is shaped throughout by the attorney's understanding of the client's goals and resources. The work process from the litigation attorney's perspective can be graphed very generally as follows:

Figure 12–2.

The typical work process for a transactional attorney has a different focus at each stage.

Input. Instead of starting with the acquisition of facts about past events, the transactional attorney usually starts with the client's proposed transaction or business planning need. Transactional attorneys are forward-looking at the beginning of the representation. They ask the client primarily about what it wants to happen rather than about what has already occurred as a prelude to applying their legal knowledge to the problem presented by the client. Professor Tina Stark describes the starting point for "deal attorneys" as follows: "Deal lawyers start from the business deal. The terms of the business deal are the deal lawyer's facts."[3]

---

[3] Tina Stark, *Thinking Like A Deal Lawyer*, 54 J. Legal Educ. 223, 224 (2004).

Analytics. Litigators take the facts they acquire and apply the law in the form of a merits evaluation that is communicated to the client. Transactional attorneys apply their knowledge of the law to the proposed deal or need of the client. The focus of this analysis is on identifying legal risks or requirements. An important part of the work of the transactional attorney is anticipating potential problems with a deal or business arrangement and designing documents or advising clients about how to avoid or manage risks associated with those potential problems.

An attorney specializing in issuance of securities, for instance, has to prepare documents that will be publicly filed describing the offering of stock or debt. The attorney has to identify the information about the company's operations that must be disclosed under federal or state securities law and craft those disclosure documents. If the client resists publicly disclosing certain information, the securities attorney's job is to counsel the client about whether the information is clearly required under the securities laws versus a disclosure made to avoid the risk of the company later being found liable for failing to reveal the information. If the disclosure is of the latter type, the attorney will advise the client as to the future legal risk of failing to make the disclosure, which the client can weigh against the disadvantages of publicly disclosing information in the present.

Deal attorneys also advise clients about the pricing of risk in a transaction. Deal attorneys evaluate proposed contract terms with an eye toward the risks that the client is being asked to assume, and the price the client is being paid (or not being paid) to assume those risks. Consider the situation of a couple building a home on a lot they own. The couple's attorney presents a proposed contract to the builder they have selected for the home. The builder rejects a provision stating that it will maintain "builder's risk insurance" covering loss by storm, fire or the like during the home construction because it costs $800. The builder contends that it is liable for any such loss and is willing to take that chance. From the couple's perspective, however, they are assuming the risk that the builder can actually perform if a storm destroys partially completed construction. The attorney has to help the clients decide whether to assume this risk, bargain with the builder to pay for the insurance, or purchase the insurance themselves.

As with litigation, the process of applying the law to the proposed deal or client need often will be an iterative dynamic between fact acquisition and legal analysis. The attorney often will identify specific legal issues when gathering facts from the client about its resources and business plans. The result of that legal research can raise questions about the client's current or anticipated conduct.

For example, think about attorneys helping a non-profit organization develop a new corporation in the form of a for-profit subsidiary to help fund its operations. The attorneys draft an initial set of documents based on the client's business plan and a meeting with the client. The attorneys, however, identify a legal risk or requirement related to the state's nonprofit corporation laws, which limits who can serve as a director of both a non-profit corporation and an affiliated for-profit corporation. The attorneys then have to acquire facts from the client about the individuals who currently serve on its board of directors and the individuals it is seeking to seat on the new board.

Product. Transactional attorneys produce documents. Deal attorneys typically draft contracts memorializing the terms agreed to by the parties to the deal. Because deal attorneys typically construct a tangible product as the end result of the representation, commentators have analogized transactional work to that of an engineer or architect.[4] Planning/Compliance attorneys draft disclosure, corporate bylaws, regulations, trust documents, and licensing registrations, and a variety of other documents. Planning/compliance attorneys also provide legal opinions, often in the form of memoranda or letters to clients or on behalf of clients to others.

Litigators, of course, also create and use documents in dispute resolution, but documents in litigation are a means to an end. When litigators file motions in litigation, for example, it is in service of the broader purpose of resolving the dispute favorably for the client. The documents created by transactional attorneys typically are the intended product of the representation.

The work process of the transactional attorney thus can be graphed roughly as follows:

Proposed Business Deal or Client Planning Need	Iterative Fact-Law Process to Identify Legal Risks or Requirements	Document that Memorializes the Deal or Meets Client Needs
INPUT	ANALYTICS	PRODUCT

Figure 12–3.

Note how problem-solving by the transactional attorney differs from that of the litigator. Transactional attorneys imagine future problems and use their legal knowledge to construct solutions to those anticipated problems or allocate the risk related to the potential future concerns.[5] Litigators

---

[4] *See, e.g.,* William J. Carney, Ronald J. Gilson and George W. Dent, *Keynote Discussion: Just Exactly What Does a Transaction Lawyer Do?,* 12 Tenn. J. Bus. L. 175 (2011).

[5] Some scholars argue that legal knowledge is not particularly central to the work of certain types of transactional attorneys. *See, e.g.,* Ronald J. Gilson, *Value Creation by Business Lawyers: Legal Skills and Asset Pricing,* 94 Yale L.J. 239, 301 (1984) (concluding as to corporate mergers

typically arrive on the scene after the dispute arises and construct strategies to achieve as favorable a resolution of the dispute as possible for the client. Professor George Dent aptly summarizes this difference as follows:

> The litigator is a soldier in battle while the transactional lawyer is a castle architect. The soldier cannot plan much in advance: no plan of battle survives the first shot. Not so the architect. She can construct the castle (or enterprise) any way she likes, but once invaders appear on the horizon it is too late to say, "Oops! I forgot to ensure a secure water supply.[6]

12.3   THE CULTURE OF TRANSACTIONAL ATTORNEYS

Transactional attorneys often describe a difference in the culture of their legal practice compared to litigators. They face a different set of incentives when relating to clients and opposing counsel or opposing parties. This section briefly describes the importance of cooperation in representing transactional clients, and describes the value of effectively managing and communicating risk assessment in transactions.

Cooperation.   Litigators mostly operate in a conflict-oriented environment. This does not mean that litigators typically are or should be contentious in style, but rather that the attorney's relationship with the client and the opposing party is shaped by the existence of parties engaged in a dispute. The culture of transactional attorneys is shaped by the fact that transactional clients reach agreements or make decisions designed to create value rather than resolve disputes.

The contrast with the litigation environment is obvious with planning/compliance attorneys because there typically is no opposite party in these matters. An attorney who works for a financial services company reviewing possible advertisements for compliance with securities and consumer protection laws does not deal with opposing counsel. This attorney may generate or have to resolve disputes with marketing employees or other parts of the company, but these are conflicts internal to the corporate client. The attorney's ability to make advertisements compliant with the governing law is enhanced when the attorney is successful at cooperating rather than accentuating conflict.

---

and acquisition work that "business lawyers play the role of transactional cost engineers, and that their historical domination of that role rests neither on its inherently legal character nor...on skills acquired through traditional legal training."). *Contrast* Stephen Schwarcz, *Explaining the Value of Transactional Lawyering*, 12 Stan. J.L. Bus. & Fin. 486 (2007) (arguing that Gilson's conclusion was incorrect and that the primary value of transactional attorneys in business deals is knowledge of regulatory law).

[6] George W. Dent, Jr., *Business Lawyers as Enterprise Architects*, 64 Bus. Law. 279, 326 (2009) (citation omitted).

Deal attorneys relate to opposing counsel or opposing parties, but this type of transactional work demands an emphasis on cooperation and trust-building, as well. Deal attorneys who bring a contentious mindset to transactional work often do so at the expense of helping the client achieve its goals. As Professors Krieger and Neumann put it, "[s]ome clients believe lawyers listen too little, dominate conversations, poison relationships by generating conflict, and raise objections when they should be developing solutions."[7] Deal attorneys can represent clients who likely have disagreements with the opposite party about the terms of a possible deal, but the goal of engaging with the other party or parties is to enter into a transaction that works for everyone.

In litigation, neither party can just abandon the dispute, unless the plaintiff concedes. Deal-making, by contrast, is voluntary. Each party needs to see a profit, a loss avoided or a risk mitigated in entering into the transaction or they won't do the deal. Attorneys representing the parties almost always will want to build trust with the opposite party when possible to help create the transaction sought by the client. When parties are able to bridge disagreements and create a transaction, they often continue the business relationship, such as when the parties are contemplating a joint venture or a lending or supplier relationship. Even in a deal to sell an asset or the like, clients often will be looking for other transactions in the future for which their reputation for cooperative conduct will be a factor. In the world of the transactional attorney, enhancing (or at least not inhibiting) trust between the parties often is an important part of the outcome of the transaction, not just a means to an end.

Attorneys as Risk-averse Deal-killers. One does not have to look very hard in most organizations, public or private, to find managers who dread the thought of involving attorneys in a potential transaction or an important decision for another reason—the unwillingness of the attorney to assume any risk. The attorney is seen as a "deal-killer" who will nitpick the terms of a transaction or raise scenarios involving future risks, however unlikely, that frighten the parties into forgoing a transaction or not taking an action. If the disagreements kill the deal, both parties have invested resources with no return.

Killing the deal may be the right result, but the job of the attorney is to help the client understand the risks of conduct, not immunize the client from risk (unless that is the client's direction). In many respects, the fear of "deal-killing" attorneys is an inevitable consequence of transactional attorneys performing their core function. As discussed in section 12.2,

---

[7] STEFAN H. KRIEGER & RICHARD K. NEUMANN, JR., ESSENTIAL LAWYERING SKILLS: INTERVIEWING, COUNSELING, NEGOTIATION, AND PERSUASIVE FACT ANALYSIS 269 (4th ed. 2011). This quote is part of an excellent discussion by Krieger and Neumann about the reasons that clients exclude lawyers from decision-making and the contribution of legal education to that result. *Id.* at 268–271.

the general analytical process for transactional attorneys centers on the anticipation of future legal risk. Transactional attorneys are supposed to imagine situations in which the deal sours or the client's preferred decision creates liability, and then help the client avoid, minimize or understand the allocation of the risk of such an event. When the deal does fall apart in the future, or when the client's decision leads to a lawsuit, the attorney likely will be at the center of any blame to be assigned. Attorneys, therefore, have an interest in contract provisions or client decisions that avoid these situations.

Therefore, risk-aversion is a natural condition for the transactional attorney because of his role as messenger of (potential) bad news. But that is only part of the problem. Attorneys in their role as planners for failure can destroy a deal over a small future risk rather than help a client create value. Very few business decisions are made without some risk involved. The transactional attorney has to objectively advise the client about the risks in a transaction or decision while building the client's trust that the attorney is trying to help the client reach a desired result. Some techniques for helping transactional attorneys achieve this balance are as follows:

(1) **Adopt a problem-solving approach when possible**. Imagine that a city government wants to hire employment counselors with federal funds allocated for crime prevention. Assume that this proposal would put the City in a legal grey area as to permissible uses of the federal money. An Assistant City Attorney is given the task of opining about whether the federal funds can be used in this manner. Think about the difference in the city officials' perception of the attorney's work product that can be implied from each of the following statements of the issue in that attorney's opinion memorandum:

Issue: Can the City Use Federal Crime Prevention Funds to Hire Employment Counselors?

Issue: What are the Risks to the City in Using Federal Crime Prevention Funds to Hire Employment Counselors?

Issue: How can the City Use Federal Crime Prevention Funds to Hire Employment Counselors?

(2) **Appreciate the existence of risk in most decision-making**. The safest approach for an attorney concerned about being held responsible if a deal or decision goes awry is to advise against any transaction or decision that involves any substantial risk. Unless the client has stated a need for a risk-free solution, this mindset will lead to unnecessary deal-killing. Instead, a transactional attorney should encourage the client to engage in a rational cost-benefit analysis of the issues. Identifying the

existence of substantial risk and clarifying the client's options for managing that risk is a different task than proceeding as if the transactional attorney's job is to eliminate risk.

The attorney does not have to agree with the decision but can respectfully point out perceived weaknesses in a client's analysis of issues. In some cases, the attorney can encourage the client to involve other people within the business entity in making decisions about a deal that the attorney believes is not in the best interests of the client. Doing so adds value to the process by bringing in the pertinent knowledge within the business organization and by getting "buy-in" and cooperation from the affected areas of the business when it comes time to perform the contractual obligations.

(3) **Understand the client and the client's business.** Deal attorneys are also business advisers. Deal attorneys need to know the client, the business that the client is engaged in and what's the "norm" for handling issues and allocating risk among the various parties to the deal in that market. Section 3.2.1 notes the importance of building trust with a client, starting with the initial interview. In the context of transactional work, it is critical to trust-building that the attorney understands the client's business or operating environment.

For example, imagine that a manufacturer of frozen desserts wants to launch an organic product line. The company hires an attorney to design its standard supply contract to ensure that it is using only organic dairy products. The attorney drafting the contract would need to understand how the organic segment of the food industry operates and how the client purchases its dairy supplies to create an effective standard contract that meets the client's stated goal. Some transactional attorneys have a regular practice of visiting the offices or other facilities of a new client, sitting through employee training sessions, or taking similar steps to familiarize themselves with the company's industry, practices and norms.

Transactional attorneys also need to understand the client before giving advice. What are unacceptable risks for one client are another client's bread and butter.

(4) **Understand the Deal or Client Need.** A litigator needs to know the case file, including the facts of the case and the course of the litigation, before appearing before a judge or making decisions about the conduct of the litigation. The same is true for transactional attorneys. A deal attorney should be able to draw a diagram that illustrates all the parties and their

relationships to each other. What are each party's goals or interests? Who has what resources to bring to the deal? You can't negotiate a deal if you don't understand it.

CHAPTER 13

NEGOTIATING TO CREATE VALUE

■ ■ ■

Effective negotiation strategy and technique depends on the context of the representation. In Chapters 8 through 11 we looked at negotiation when the attorney is representing a client in perhaps the most common type of litigation—a dispute over a loss as a result of past conduct in which the parties have no interest in a continuing relationship. Representation in most transaction matters (and many cases in litigation) can be more effective if the attorney helps create value for the client through the use of integrative negotiation techniques.[1]

Section 13.1 introduces the basics of integrative negotiations and how this approach differs from the tasks facing an attorney engaged in distributive negotiations. Section 13.2 examines when and how to use integrative as opposed to distributive negotiation methods, and the difficult job of simultaneously applying both negotiation approaches in the same matter. Section 13.3 notes special concerns in managing two party negotiations with multiple issues to resolve.

13.1   BASIC PRINCIPLES OF INTEGRATIVE NEGOTIATION

In an influential book on negotiating, *Getting to Yes*, Roger Fisher and William Ury promise readers that using their "principled negotiation" method "permits you to reach a gradual consensus on a joint decision efficiently without all the transactional costs of digging in to positions only to have to dig yourself out of them."[2] Their cooperative and problem-solving approach to negotiation also has been called "integrative negotiation."[3]   This section discusses two basic concepts underlying integrative negotiation: creating rather than distributing value in

---

[1] This section continues the focus on two party negotiations. The dynamics of negotiation can change substantially when the matter involves multiple parties. *See* HOWARD RAIFFA, THE ART AND SCIENCE OF NEGOTIATION 257–334 (1982).

[2] ROGER FISHER & WILLIAM L. URY, GETTING TO YES 14 (1981).

[3] Lieb Leventhal traces the concepts underlying integrative negotiation to the published work of Mary Parker Follett in the early 1900s. Lieb Leventhal, *Implementing Interest-Based Negotiation: Conditions for Success with Evidence from Kaiser Permanente*, 61 DISP. RESOL. J. 50 (2006).

negotiations, and employing a cooperative rather than adversarial approach to negotiating.

13.1.1   CREATING VALUE

The touchstone of integrative negotiations is that parties in negotiation can create value through the negotiating process rather than just distribute value or loss. The goal of the integrative negotiator is to search for some form of "win-win" result in which each party can achieve some or all of its primary goals in a settlement. This approach to negotiations is predicated on the notion that the goals of the parties to the negotiation are not mutually exclusive.

A key insight of integrative negotiation theory is that parties can achieve a mutually beneficial outcome by shifting the focus of discussion from the conflicting positions of the parties to the individual interests of the parties in the matter underlying the negotiation. Consider two neighbors, Quong (who has lived there for 35 years) and Bailey (the new resident). They have a tall shrub planted on the property line in their back yard, which looks something like this:

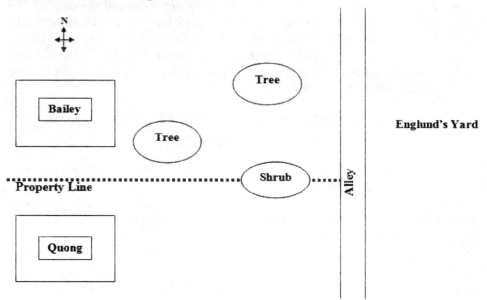

Figure 13–1.

Bailey wants to keep the shrub trimmed low and Quong wants the shrub as tall as possible. They argue: "short," "tall," "Short," "Tall," "SHORT!," "TALL!." These are the competing positions of the two neighbors.

Integrative negotiation theory suggests asking each party to identify his interest in the height of the shrub; i.e., why does Bailey want it trimmed short and why does Quong want it left tall? Bailey's interest in the height of the shrub is that it allows sunlight to the only part of his yard that is not otherwise shaded so that he can grow vegetables. Quong wants the shrub left tall because a tall shrub blocks the view of the yard across the alley owned by Englund; a yard that Quong finds unsightly. This shift from the seemingly irreconcilable positions of the parties to the underlying interests of the parties in the matter of dispute is critical to employing integrative negotiating to attempt to resolve the problem.[4]

Once the parties identify their interests, integrative negotiators begin to look for solutions that will meet the interests of both parties. The focus of this search for alternatives is on solutions, not on the conflict. In the case of Bailey and Quong, this means that the search for a solution should focus on Bailey's interest in a sunny garden space and Quong's interest in blocking the view of the messy neighbors. Neither Bailey nor Quong need give up their respective interest in searching for a solution, but both have to be flexible about the method for meeting those interests rather than fixating on the shrub height as the only means of achieving their respective goals.

Quong and Bailey talk. After thinking of various options for meeting the needs at hand, Quong has an idea. Bailey's enthusiasm for fresh vegetables has kindled Quong's interest in vegetable gardening. His deceased wife was a great gardener and he eventually gave up trying to keep her garden planted because he "has a brown thumb," so he planted over that part of his sunny yard with grass. Quong offers that Bailey can plant vegetables in Quong's yard. Bailey finds that solution preferable to having a vegetable garden in his yard. Bailey can use that space for other things, and is happy to keep the shrub as tall as Quong wants it to grow. They agree to share the harvest from the garden.

13.1.2 COOPERATIVE AND OPEN–MINDED APPROACH

A corollary in integrative negotiations for the switch in perspective from distributing value to creating value is the switch from an adversarial style of negotiating to a cooperative approach.[5] Integrative negotiation theorists encourage parties to approach negotiation as a joint problem to be solved, if possible, through cooperative idea generation and evaluation of alternative solutions to that problem.

Cooperative problem-solving requires a mutual exchange of information— a characteristic often considered a hallmark of the integrative negotiation

---

[4] Section 13.2.1 examines the identification of interests in more detail.

[5] For more in-depth analysis of negotiation styles, see STEFAN H KRIEGER & RICHARD K. NEUMANN, JR., ESSENTIAL LAWYERING SKILLS: INTERVIEWING, COUNSELING, NEGOTIATION, AND PERSUASIVE FACT ANALYSIS (4TH ED. 2011). *See, e.g.,* Melissa L. Nelken, *The Myth of the Gladiator and Law Students: Negotiation Styles,* 7 CARDOZO J. CONFLICT RESOL. 1 (2005) (discussing competitive, collaborative, accommodating, avoidance, and compromising styles of negotiation); Charles B Craver, *Negotiation Styles the Impact on Bargaining Transactions,* 58 DISP. RESOL. J. 48 (2003) (analyzing competitive, cooperative and hybrid negotiation styles).

approach. Successful negotiations between Quong and Bailey were possible only because they were willing to share information about their interests and work together on possible solutions to the dispute. Professor Roy Lewicki and colleagues describe integrative negotiations as involving "a free flow of information."[6] They observe that:

> Ample research evidence indicates that effective information exchange promotes the development of good integrative solutions. Researchers have shown that the failure to reach integrative agreements is often linked to the failure to exchange enough information to allow the parties to identify integrative options...[N]egotiators must create the conditions for a free and open discussion of all related issues and concerns. Willingness to share information is not a characteristic of distributive bargaining situations, in which parties distrust one another, conceal and manipulate information, and attempt to learn about the other for their own competitive advantage.[7]

In addition to a cooperative view of negotiations, integrative theorists encourage parties to approach negotiation with an open-mind. Fisher and Ury warn against starting negotiations with a mindset that limits creative problem-solving. They identify "four major obstacles that inhibit the inventing of an abundance of options," as follows: (1) prematurely judging the limits of possible solutions; (2) trying to identify one best answer rather than create options for evaluation; (3) assuming the situation requires bargaining over a fixed amount; and (4) concern only with the party's own interests rather than working to help meet the other party's interests.[8]

13.2   USING INTEGRATIVE NEGOTIATIONS IN LEGAL REPRESENTATION

Both sides winning (at least partly), a more cooperative and less adversarial process, and expanding available resources by creating value in negotiations—why would anyone engage in old-style distributive negotiations? Despite the appeal of the integrative negotiating method, it is not constructive for reaching the goals of the legal client in many situations. In some cases, naively negotiating with a cooperative and problem-solving mindset can leave the attorney, and her client, open to exploitation.

This section examines when attorneys can effectively use integrative negotiating. Section 13.2.1 looks at the tension that arises when one party approaches negotiations as zero-sum and the other party attempts

---

[6] ROY J. LEWICKI, ET AL., NEGOTIATION (3rd ed. 1999).

[7] *Id.* at 108 (citations omitted).

[8] FISHER & Ury, *supra* note 2, at 57–59.

to use cooperative negotiation methods. Section 13.2.2 discusses how to recognize situations commonly facing attorneys in which integrative negotiations are most likely to succeed. And section 13.2.3 briefly looks at how to implement integrative negotiating approaches in legal matters.

13.2.1 TENSION BETWEEN CREATING VALUE AND DISTRIBUTING VALUE

Because integrative negotiations are generally characterized by open information sharing and a cooperative approach to problem-solving, the integrative negotiator will not succeed in creating value unless she knows the interests that both sides have in the matter being negotiated. Recall that in distributive negotiations the bargaining parties use anchoring offers, concession patterns and accompanying presentation of offers as a way of signaling whether a deal is possible. The distributive negotiator tries to hide his bottom line. He will utterly fail at obtaining the best deal if he gives away information that leads the other party to discover his reservation price at the beginning of the negotiation.

The problem for the negotiator is deciding when to freely share information in support of creating value and when to hide information in support of getting the best deal in distributing value. Professor Robert Mnookin and colleagues describe this tension between creating and distributing value as follows: "without sharing information it is difficult to create value, but when disclosure is one-sided, the disclosing party risks being taken advantage of."[9] As Professor William Carney explains it:

> The problem is that creating value, the win-win concept that is both right and incomplete in critical respect, and dividing it, the distributive bargaining element, take place at exactly the same time. At the same time everyone is talking about how to cooperate to make the transaction succeed, they are also anticipating how the success is going to be shared, and all other things equal, each party wants more. The difficulty caused by the simultaneous creation and division of value is that a lot of the techniques we use to create value—for example, open and honest sharing of what our needs are, what things we value,

---

[9] ROBERT H. MNOOKIN, ET AL., BEYOND WINNING: NEGOTIATING TO CREATE VALUE IN DEALS AND DISPUTES (2000). Most negotiating theory expressly or impliedly advocates for a cooperative rather than adversarial style by negotiators. For an excellent summary of the literature on differing styles in negotiation and the need to think contextually about negotiating style in law, *see* Andrea K. Schneider, *Teaching a New Negotiating Skills Paradigm*, 39 WASH. U. J. L. & POL'Y 13 (2012).

honest collaboration—can profoundly reduce the ability to engage in distributive bargaining.[10]

This tension between distributing and creating value in negotiations is supported by research from social psychologists establishing that most people approach negotiation situations with "fixed-pie" assumptions; that is, with a distributive negotiation mindset.[11]

Imagine an example involving the purchase of an historic home. Barbara has a 19th century home she is trying to restore with impeccable historical accuracy. The project demands a rare set of fixtures—woodwork and chandeliers—that complement similar fixtures already in her home. Barbara discovers a deteriorated home for sale on Dayton Avenue in her neighborhood that has both the rare woodwork and the rare chandeliers. Barbara offers the homeowner $20,000 to purchase the desired fixtures in the Dayton Avenue home, but the homeowner is uninterested in selling only the fixtures. Barbara can buy the house, take out and replace the fixtures, and then resell the home, but that option involves substantial transaction costs. That deal probably would cost Barbara $30,000 by the time she buys and resells the house, as well as consume a lot of her time and subject her to risk. Barbara's alternative for acquiring the fixtures is to purchase similar fixtures from a specialty supplier at a cost of more than $40,000, and those fixtures are of lower quality than the fixtures in the Dayton Avenue home.

Iglehart Ventures is a small enterprise interested in purchasing the Dayton Avenue home for rehabilitation and resale. Iglehart appreciates the fixtures, but it is unaware that they are unusually rare items and it does not consider them crucial to its project. It could replace the fixtures with similar items at a cost of no more than $5,000. Iglehart's primary concern is its cash position. Iglehart is worried that buying and remodeling the home will drain all of its cash and force it to create more debt than it wants to hold.

Hopefully, you are getting the knack of integrative negotiation theory and see a possible deal (or multiple options for a deal) to create value for both Barbara and Iglehart. Barbara wants the fixtures; Iglehart wants the house. Barbara, for instance, could agree to give $20,000 to Iglehart for the fixtures when it closes on the house, thus providing Iglehart with a net $15,000 in up-front capital ($20,000 for the fixtures minus the $5,000 replacement cost). There could be other options that would work for both parties. Barbara hears that Iglehart is the other interested buyer for the house. What should Barbara say to Iglehart for the purpose of obtaining the fixtures?

---

[10] William Carney, et. al., *Keynote Discussion: Just Exactly What Does A Transaction Lawyer Do?*, 15 Tenn. J. Bus. Law 175, 177 (2011).

[11] Leigh Thompson & Reid Hastie, *Social Perception in Negotiation*, 47 ORGANIZATIONAL BEHAV. & HUM. DECISION PROCESSES 98 (1990).

Barbara is caught in the tension between creating and distributing value. If Barbara tells Iglehart that her interest in the house is solely to obtain the fixtures, negative consequences could result. Iglehart likely would realize it had not seen the value in the fixtures. It might compete more aggressively with Barbara for the house and then try to sell the fixtures to Barbara at a price of up to $40,000 if it prevails. Worse yet, Iglehart might sell the fixtures to another buyer or it might keep the fixtures and use their value to raise the resale price of the home. All of these choices probably look worse to Barbara than just buying and reselling the home.

On the other hand, Barbara has little chance of reaching a deal that creates value for both parties unless she reveals her unique interest in the Dayton Avenue house. Barbara can't create value without sharing her underlying interests with Iglehart, but disclosing her interests exposes her to the risk of being on the wrong end of distributive bargaining with Iglehart.

13.2.2 CONDITIONS CONDUCIVE TO INTEGRATIVE NEGOTIATIONS

Many negotiation situations suggest the use of some distributive bargaining and some integrative negotiating techniques. The attorney must recognize which negotiating approach is likely to be most effective for the client in each particular matter (or, to make things more complicated, for each discrete issue within each matter). Professor Mnookin and colleagues argue that tension between creating and distributing value in negotiations is a problem to be managed rather than resolved. The goal is to negotiate in a way "that allow(s) value creation to occur, when possible, while minimizing the risks of exploitation."[12]

Below are four factors to consider when determining whether an integrative or distributive approach is more likely to be productive for achieving the client's interests in legal negotiations.

1. Do the parties have a mutual interest in a continuing relationship?

Parties that will be forced to work together in the future, or who want to create or continue a productive relationship, are more likely to benefit from integrative negotiations. Most marital dissolutions involving children merit integrative approaches, at least as to the parenting arrangements. On the other hand, the

---

[12] MNOOKIN ET AL., *supra* note 11, at 27. For a review of the literature on managing the tension between distributive and integrative negotiation, see Claude Alavoine, *Ethics in Negotiations: The Confrontation Between Representation and* Practices, 54 WORLD ACAD. SCI. ENGINEERING & TECH. 205, 206 (2011), *available at* www.waset.org/journals/waset/v54/v54-40.pdf (observing that "managing the dilemma between these two [negotiating] processes present a central challenge to negotiators.").

victims of the gas leak case described in chapter 2 are unlikely to have any regard for a continuing relationship with the company that owns the chemical plant.

Revisit with a twist the situation facing Barbara in dealing with Iglehart Ventures. What if Iglehart is owned by a person who lives on Barbara's block and whose children are good friends with Barbara's children? This might give Barbara a sense of trust in approaching Iglehart's owner about a possible win-win deal (of course, it might also make Barbara want to walk away from the deal for fear of social complications).

2. Do the parties have complementary interests or resources?

Parties can identify and use complementary interests and resources to reach an integrative solution. This is the "Jack Sprat" element of integrative negotiating. In the example above involving Barbara and Iglehart, one wanted fixtures and the other wanted the remainder of the house.

Section 13.3 looks at counseling clients to create options for integrative solutions. Throughout the negotiation process the attorney should be carefully listening for interests and resources of the client and the other party that can be paired to create integrative solutions to some or all of the issues presented in the negotiation. Finding an integrative solution to what appeared to the parties to be a distributive problem can be one of the most satisfying and trust-building aspects of the attorney-client relationship.

3. Do the parties need to reach an agreement to achieve an important interest in the matter?

Parties who need to reach an agreement to achieve their interests are more likely to invest in integrative negotiations. This is one of the reasons that transaction attorneys should generally be more likely to employ integrative negotiations when working on a possible deal while litigators are more likely to rely on distributive negotiations. Failure to reach a deal in a transaction probably means the parties have wasted substantial efforts with nothing to show for it. Typically, failure to settle a lawsuit just means the parties are back to the litigation position they were in prior to settlement talks.

4. What are the costs of integrative negotiations?

Integrative negotiations generally require higher costs. The parties need to discuss their interests in the matter, and work creatively to investigate possible mutually beneficial solutions. These actions use time and resources, but also can result in a better bargain. Integrative negotiations, therefore, can be especially profitable when the costs of negotiating in this manner are more than offset by the potential for a superior deal.[13]

In legal negotiations, it is obvious that the prototypical transactional matter is more likely to be amenable to a cooperative approach than is the prototypical litigation dispute, for the reasons mentioned in section 11.3. When two parties meet to discuss working together, such as businesses discussing a joint venture, the parties are especially likely to be disposed to sharing information and working toward a mutually beneficial solution. Yet most negotiations have some element of distributing value, as well. Two businesses talking about a joint venture eventually will have to discuss the capital contributions to, control over and percentage ownership in the joint venture.

Conversely, litigation sometimes can be resolved by applying integrative techniques. A wrongful death action against a hospital would seem to present a classic distributive negotiation problem—no continuing relationship, no obvious complementary interests, etc. Yet the client may have objectives that allow for integrative negotiations. For example, a case involving a child who died after routine surgery may leave the parents angry and grief-stricken and wanting to recover a large award of damages from the hospital. But some parents may also be interested in leaving a legacy that will commemorate their child by establishing a fund for the hospital to use to buy equipment, train staff or study new procedures that will reduce the chance of other similar tragedies.

13.2.3 IMPLEMENTING INTEGRATIVE LEGAL NEGOTIATIONS

This subsection elaborates three concepts that integrative negotiation theorists have described as part of a mindset of negotiators who effectively employ integrative negotiation practices.

Express a Problem-solving Approach. The biggest obstacle to creating value through integrative negotiations when conditions favor such negotiations is that opposing parties usually default to an assumption that the negotiation is about distributing existing value. As a cross-disciplinary team of researchers at Tilburg University put it, "[a]dhering to one's initial belief that the other party's interests are opposed to one's own requires less effort than adjusting one's expectations."[14] One tactic

---

[13] Of course, distributive negotiations run amok can prolong costly litigation or cause profitable deals to be lost.

[14] Laura Klaming, et al., *I Want the Opposite of What You Want: Reducing Fixed-Pie Perceptions in Online Negotiations*, 2009 J. Disp. Resol. 139, 143 (2009). The Tilburg researchers also observe that negotiating parties tend to retain this perception even as new information might be thought to suggest an alternative approach: "In addition to a reluctance to put more effort into understanding the opponent's priorities, people tend to hold onto their earlier beliefs and seek information that is consistent with, rather than conflicting with, these beliefs. Because

for changing this default is to project a problem-solving attitude toward the negotiations. State an interest in hearing the other party's perspective on the problem. Consider beginning negotiations by expressly stating an interest in a problem-solving approach. As Professor James Holbrook puts it, "[a] party's opening statement can strongly suggest the type of solution he is seeking. Opening remarks communicating interest in both the outcome of the negotiation and the relationship with the other party signal a desire for a more integrative solution."[15]

Cultivate Reciprocity. Building a process that encourages open exchange of information requires trust that the information exchange will be mutual. Negotiators concerned about adverse consequences from sharing information can encourage reciprocity by sharing some information and then gauging the response from the other side. The process of reciprocal exchange has been described as follows: "The process begins when at least one participant makes a move, and if the other reciprocates, new rounds of exchange initiate. Once the process is in motion, each consequence can create a self-reinforcing cycle."[16]

Separate the People from the Problem. Fisher and Ury emphasize the importance of separating the human relationship between the negotiating parties and the substance of the matter about which they are negotiating. "A basic fact about negotiation, easy to forget in corporate and international transactions, is that you are dealing not with abstract representatives of the 'other side,' but with human beings. They have emotions, deeply held values and different backgrounds and viewpoints, and they are unpredictable. So are you."[17]

That this observation may seem self-evident doesn't stop problems that arise from the parties' emotional investment in the negotiations from being a common reason for negotiations to fail. Negotiators become enmeshed in the substance of the dispute and disagreements over the substance can conflate with opposition to "giving in" to an outcome perceived as favoring the other party.[18] Distributive negotiations often reinforce this problem. As Fisher and Ury suggest, "[f]raming a negotiation as a contest of wills over position aggravates the entangling

---

cognitive resources are limited, focusing on achieving a favorable outcome often conflicts with comprehending the opponent's preferences." *Id.*

[15] James R. Holbrook, *Using Performative, Distributive, Integrative, and Transformative Principles in Negotiation*, 56 LOY. L. REV. 359, 365 (2010).

[16] Russell Cropanzano & Marie S. Mitchell, 31 J. MGMT. 874, 876 (2005). Professors Cropanzano and Mitchell describe this type of reciprocity as "interdependent reciprocity." Their article also describes two other types of norms of reciprocal behavior and provides a review of the literature in this area. *Id.* at 875–78.

[17] FISHER & Ury, *supra* note 2, at 18–19.

[18] One of the reasons that parties in a dispute often successfully resolve the matter during mediation is that the presence of a third party can diffuse the problems that arise from people-driven obstacles to settlement rather than issues inherent in problem resolution.

process."[19] They encourage negotiators to separate the substance of the problem from the relationship of the negotiating parties, urging negotiators to "[d]eal with people problems directly; don't try to solve them with substantive concessions."[20]

13.3   NEGOTIATING IN A MULTI–ISSUE ENVIRONMENT

This section examines an issue that occurs in both distributive and integrative negotiations—how to negotiate when the matter involves multiple issues, interests, goals or factors. A dispute between an insurer and insured over payment from storm damage usually involves just a question of how much the insurer will pay to the insured. The typical transaction matter and a substantial percentage of disputes require the parties to resolve multiple concerns. An agreement to lease space at a mall will force the parties to settle on a monthly rent amount, but this agreement also may concern excluding similar retailers from nearby space, promotion of the business of the lessee by the mall, the question of who pays for certain improvements to the space, and other issues.

This section looks at the problem of sequencing the order of items discussed in multi-issue negotiations. If two parties have a range of issues to resolve in reaching a deal, where do you start? The process used by the negotiators likely will affect the tenor and outcome of the talks. Commentators suggest that parties involved in multi-issue negotiations can take one of the three following approaches for the order of discussing issues in negotiation.[21]

> First, the parties can approach negotiation as a **package deal**. The parties treat all the issues as a bundle and do not discuss issues independently. Under this approach one party would present all of its proposed terms to resolve each of the issues and the other party would respond with its proposed terms on all of the issues.

> Second, the parties can engage in **simultaneous negotiation** of the issues. The parties address each issue independently but defer final resolution on any particular issue until resolution is reached on all issues.

---

[19] FISHER & URY, *supra* note 2, at 20–21.

[20] FISHER & URY, *supra* note 2, at 21.

[21] *See, e.g.*, Shaheen S. Fatima, et al., *Multi-Issue Negotiation with Deadlines*, 27 J. ARTIFICIAL INTELLIGENCE RES. 381, 382 (2006), *available at* http://arxiv.org/pdf/1110.2765.pdf. Much of the scholarship in this area relies heavily on mathematical analysis an effort to determine efficient negotiating processes. *See also, e.g.*, Joao de Oliveira & Marek Karczewski, *Comparison of Multi-Issue Negotiation Techniques for Constructing Intelligent Distributed Systems*, SCRIBD, http://www.scribd.com/doc/11473452/MultiIssue-Negotiation-Paper (last visited Mar. 18, 2013); RAIFFA, *supra* note 1, at 133–250.

Third, the parties can negotiate each issue in a **sequential** order, reaching resolution on one issue and then moving to the next until everything is resolved.

As with the exercise of many professional skills by an attorney, there is no correct answer among these choices that applies to all situations. But just proceeding without thinking about the likely optimal process for the situation at hand is ill-advised. The attorney should make a conscious choice about whether to open negotiations with a discussion of process or just proceed with one approach or another.

Consider the negotiating terrain common in certain types of public agency civil law enforcement actions. For example, a case by the United States Consumer Financial Protection Bureau ("CFPB") against a bank it alleges misled customers in selling a privacy protection program billed on customer credit cards. Or a state environmental protection agency that alleges that a company operating a petroleum transfer station allowed its storage tanks to leak toxins into the groundwater. Such agency enforcement actions often have several or all of the following components to address in negotiation: (1) an injunction to prevent or constrain the company's conduct in the future; (2) a civil monetary penalty paid to the government; (3) remediation of the harm, such as restitution payments to consumers or groundwater clean-up; and (4) the form of the settlement, such as whether it must be court-approved and whether it will be a public document.

Let's look at some of the reasons that parties to these types of negotiations may prefer to use or avoid each of the three methods for ordering the discussion. An advantage of the package deal process, and to a lesser extent the simultaneous process, is that parties will not be surprised by information or demands on a later issue that would change impressions of a deal reached on earlier-discussed issue. A company accused of illegal discharge of toxins may care most about financial cost. If the company agrees to a civil penalty and remediation costs, but then discovers that the state environmental agency is demanding installation of expensive new equipment as part of the injunction covering future conduct, the company may want to re-open discussion of the amounts it will pay for a penalty and remediation. Conversely, if the company mainly wants to avoid bad publicity, its attorney may suggest the sequential approach to see if the company can obtain a confidentiality order before it broaches the other concerns.

The parties also may have information or interests that favor a certain approach. For instance, the bank in the CFPB case may be ready to discontinue its sale of the privacy protection product for reasons completely separate from the regulator's concerns. That means the bank likely cares little about future restrictions on the marketing of the product. In this case, the bank probably considers simultaneous negotiations ideal because it can give ground on the injunction in favor of other issues; by discussing all the issues independently but simultaneously it is most likely to obtain value for its apparent "concessions." Alternatively, the CFPB and the bank may have had tense interactions in the past leading to mistrust. Sequential negotiations may be a way to resolve an "easy" issue first, thus allowing both sides to build confidence and trust for addressing the other concerns under discussion.

Parties can combine approaches to create a hybrid negotiating process that fits the circumstances. In the case of the public agency civil enforcement actions, for instance, it might make sense to negotiate sequentially overall, but to treat the civil penalty and remediation issues simultaneously, as they both involve money payments.

CHAPTER 14

CLIENT COUNSELING AND RELATIONSHIPS

■ ■ ■

The focus of this chapter is counseling the client in preparation for negotiations. Section 11.2 looked at client counseling in the context of mediation in a litigation matter involving solely distributive concerns. We return to client counseling in the more demanding environment of multiple issues for discussion with the possibility of creating value through the negotiation process.

Section 14.1 briefly looks at the formation of the attorney-client relationship and control of decision-making in the relationship. Section 14.2 turns attention to the information that the attorney will need from the client to engage in effective counseling prior to negotiations that may have integrative elements. Section 14.3 looks at the process of working with the client to generate and evaluate options for creating a deal or resolving a dispute.

14.1 ATTORNEY–CLIENT RELATIONSHIP REVISITED

The work of an attorney who represents an individual or organizational client is defined by the attorney's relationship with the client. Chapter 6 introduced the boundaries of the attorney-client relationship defined by the ethical rules circumscribing the actions of attorneys. This section highlights three aspects of that relationship important for completing the transaction simulation—formalizing the attorney-client relationship, discussing confidentiality with the client, and the scope of client-delegated authority.

14.1.1 FORMATION OF RELATIONSHIP

The attorney-client relationship can be formed even in the absence of a written agreement.[1] Nonetheless, it is almost always advisable to reduce

---

[1] First Hawaiian Bank v. Russell & Volkening, Inc., 861 F.Supp. 233, 238 (S.D.N.Y. 1994) (noting that the existence of a written retainer agreement is one factor in a multi-part test to determine the existence of an attorney-client relationship). In some situations, professional responsibility rules or other statutes require that the relationship be committed to writing. *See, e.g.,* MODEL RULES OF PROF'L CONDUCT, R. 1.5 (2011); MCK. CONSOL. LAWS, BOOK 29 APP., N.Y. ST RPC R. 1.3 (McKinney 2012).

the representation to writing as soon as practical. Attorneys refer to this writing as a "retainer agreement." Money paid up front to secure the fee of the attorneys or costs anticipated in the representation is commonly called a "retainer fee."[2]

Retainer agreements, as with most contracts, will vary substantially depending on the area of law, the type of client, the compensation arrangements and the style of the attorney. Most retainer agreements will contain the following elements:

* *Scope of Service.* The agreement will identify the exact matter on which the attorney will provide representation and disclaim any responsibility for representing the client beyond the identified scope.

* *Fee Arrangement.* The agreement will specify how the client will pay the attorney or how the attorney will otherwise be compensated. If the client is responsible for a flat fee or hourly charge for the service, the agreement will state how the client will be billed and the payment terms. If the attorney will be compensated by a percentage of any recovery (contingency fee) or in a similar manner, the agreement will state the specific terms for the determination of the attorney's charge, such as whether the percentage will be determined before or after the recovery of costs.

* *Duties and Rights of Withdrawal.* The agreement will specify the obligations of the attorney in providing the service and the obligations of the client to assist in the representation. The agreement also will reserve the attorney's right to withdraw from the representation under certain circumstances.

* *No Guarantee.* Often, the agreement will include a disclaimer about the results of the representation, such as a statement that the attorney has not guaranteed a particular outcome in the matter.

The attorney will review the key terms of the retainer agreement with the client, and obtain the client's signature on the agreement, before providing advice to the client or stating to others that the attorney represents the client.

14.1.2 EXPLAINING CONFIDENTIALITY

The other routine task performed by most attorneys at the outset of the relationship is to explain the contours and importance of confidentiality of

---

[2] *See* Donna G. Mcgee, Comment, *Interpretation of Retainers and Contingent Fee Arrangements*, 25 J. LEGAL PROF. 195 (2001) (describing different forms of retainer fees).

communications.[3] Attorneys talk to clients about confidentiality both to promote disclosure and to prevent destruction of the privilege. The attorney wants the client to be honest and reveal all relevant information about the representation. Clients who understand that the attorney is obligated to keep information confidential presumably are more willing to share information fully and honestly.

Attorneys regularly assure their clients that the information they communicate to the attorney will be held in confidence because the attorney is under a legal obligation not to disclose the client's communications to anyone, including testifying in court. *See* Section 6.3.4. And this is true, mostly. There are six exceptions to attorney confidentiality in the Model Rules of Professional Conduct, such as to prevent the client from committing certain types of crimes.[4] Although there is scholarly disagreement about the detail with which attorneys should discuss these exceptions with their clients at the start of the relationship, most commentators take the approach that the attorney should mention the existence of these exceptions generally rather than provide an exhaustive explanation of the exceptions.[5]

The attorney also wants the client to understand that confidentiality is a two-way street. Attorneys hold client communications in confidence, and the client should be careful not to disclose the attorney-client communication to others. Telling others about the attorney's statements to the client, or about the communications between the attorney and client, might mean that the communications will no longer be protected by law.

Thus, the attorney should present the concept of attorney-client confidentiality by describing the legal obligation of the attorney to keep client communications in confidence, by mentioning at least generally that there might be exceptions, and by stressing that clients should also be vigilant in not revealing communications from and with the attorney. Putting this together, the following is an example of one effective way to communicate this information:

---

[3] Leslie C. Levin, *Testing the Radical Experiment: A Study of Lawyer Response to Clients Who Intend to Harm* Others, 47 RUTGERS L. REV. 81, 120–21 (reporting results of a survey of New Jersey attorneys showing that 95% of attorneys had informed at least some of their clients about confidentiality of communications, although discussion of confidentiality was found much more frequently among attorneys practicing criminal law).

[4] MODEL RULES OF PROF'L CONDUCT, R. 1.6 (2011). "A lawyer may reveal information relating to the representation of a client to the extent the lawyer reasonably believes necessary...(2) to prevent the client from committing a crime or fraud that is reasonably certain to result in substantial injury to the financial interests or property of another and in furtherance of which the client has used or is using the lawyer's services."

[5] Elisia M. Klinka & Russell G Pearce, *Confidentiality Explained: The Dialogue Approach to Discussing Confidentiality with* Clients, 48 SAN DIEGO L. REV. 157, 184–98 (2011) (explicating different proposed arguments about how to discuss confidentiality exceptions with clients).

You may have heard about attorney-client confidentiality, and I want to talk to you briefly about the importance of this law. It means that I cannot tell anyone else what you say to me. There are a few exceptions to this rule, but I do not think they will arise in this case and I will tell you if I think those situations might be happening. I need you to be open and honest in telling me about your situation.

What I tell you also is confidential, so long as no else finds out about what we discuss. It is very important that you not discuss with others what we talk about or any letters I send you or the like—this means not talking about our communications even with your spouse or best friend. Do you have any questions about my responsibilities or your responsibilities to keep our communications confidential?

14.1.3 SCOPE OF DELEGATED NEGOTIATING AUTHORITY

Recall from Chapter 6 that one of the 5 C's of the ethical rules for attorneys is "client control." The client is in charge of the objectives of the representation and must authorize the terms of settlement in negotiations. When present at a negotiation, the client can easily control the offer terms and the amount or type of concessions. A lot of negotiating between attorneys, however, occurs outside the presence of the client. In this situation, it is critical that the attorney be cognizant of the scope of her negotiating authority.

Because attorneys are agents of their clients, they can bind clients to agreements reached in a negotiation. The attorney, therefore, cannot agree to any term of a settlement unless the attorney knows that the client has fully authorized agreement on that term. A client who is an author might instruct her attorney who is negotiating a cash advance as follows, "I will accept a $75,000 advance for the book, but it has to be up front—no payments over two or three years." The author's attorney receives the following offer during a phone call with the publisher's attorney, "We are delighted to offer your client an advance of $100,000. We can provide one-fourth of that amount immediately and pay the remainder in three equal installments every two months for the next six months." This deal is very likely acceptable to the author, but her attorney does not have the authority to accept the deal. The attorney has authority to accept the amount of the advance, but not the timing of the payments, even though the client's concern was about payments stretching over years, not months.

This need for clarity of authority has obvious implications for client counseling. The attorney needs to be quite precise about what the client has or has not agreed to regarding the attorney's authority to bind the client on specific terms.

14.2   PLANNING FOR INTEGRATIVE NEGOTIATIONS

Preparation for negotiations that may use integrative techniques requires working closely with the client to undercover the client's underlying needs and priorities, as well as other important information. Section 14.2.1 discusses identifying the client's interests prior to engaging in integrative negotiations.   Section 14.2.2 examines how to employ the concept of BATNA in negotiations that go beyond recovery or payment of money to resolve a distributive problem. Section 14.2.3 discusses the advantages of taking an inventory of each party's resources and rights.

14.2.1   IDENTIFYING INTERESTS

Integrative negotiation is sometimes called "interest-based negotiation." The identification of each party's underlying interests, as opposed to their positions, is an indispensible step in this negotiation method.

Section 3.1 introduced working with the client to identify goals. A client's goals, whether monetary or non-monetary, are about a desired outcome from litigation or from a negotiated agreement. The client's goals can usually be tied directly to the client's positions in the matter. The goal of recovering the complete loss of a building from a fire can lead to a position of not taking less than $500,000 in negotiations with the insurer (i.e., a reservation price). A client's interests relate to the client's fears, needs, concerns or hopes concerning the matter.

In some cases, this distinction is of little consequence. A sole proprietor who owns a profitable building materials distribution company may be ready to retire and sell her operation. This person's goal might be to make the most money from the sale and complete the transaction as quickly as possible.   These goals of the client probably elucidate negotiating strategy better than re-framing the situation in terms of interests (e.g., supporting an affluent retirement lifestyle and fear of having to work extra years while awaiting a sale).

In other cases, the difference between goals and interests is the difference between helping the client create a more effective approach to negotiation and taking the path of least resistance in the negotiation. Consider the same scenario with the sale of a distribution business by a sole proprietor. In this situation, however, the proprietor has the following multiple interests in the matter: supporting an affluent retirement lifestyle, rewarding and considering the needs of several long-term employees of the business, protecting or enhancing her reputation in the community, and having some continued role in the building industry after the sale of the company. It is difficult to reduce this list of interests to outcome-oriented goals without understanding the possibilities that will open up in negotiating with various potential buyers.

Identifying the interests of the client often requires effort beyond a simple inquiry. If Mr. Quong, the homeowner introduced in Section 13.1.1, was asked by an attorney, "What do you want to happen with this dispute over the shrub?," it is likely Mr. Quong would tell the attorney he wants a taller shrub. To determine Mr. Quong's underlying interest in the shrub, the attorney will need to ask why—"Why do you want a taller shrub?" In response to this question, Mr. Quong may say, "Because it looks better from my yard that way." Again, to get to Mr. Quong's underlying interest that will help resolve the matter, the attorney will have to dig deeper to discover that he is worried about the view of the messy neighbor across the alley.[6]

In most cases, the client will have more than one interest in the matter. As discussed in Section 3.1, an attorney needs to communicate with the client to create as detailed a ranking, or gauge as clearly as possible, the client's priorities among multiple goals. The same is true with interests.

14.2.2 BATNA

BATNA stands for "Best Alternative to Negotiated Agreement." In Section 8.1.1, we discussed the concept of reservation price as a particular application of BATNA to the situation facing an attorney in distributive negotiations in litigation over past money loss, where the alternative to settling is continued litigation. In most transactional matters, and many litigated cases, the BATNA concept has a broader meaning. BATNA asks the person in negotiations to identify her preferred alternative action if the parties fail to conclude a deal in negotiations.

A well-prepared party needs a BATNA in integrative negotiations. While the purpose of this type of negotiation is to create value in the process, the discussion of alternatives still should be grounded by the comparison between possible negotiated terms and the best alternative to those terms.

Let's return to the Nowecki case. Prior to having a dispute over the breach of a three-year supply contract, 3C and Nowecki negotiated the terms of that contract. Nowecki would have been in the best position to negotiate that contract if it identified its BATNA before reaching a deal with 3C. Assuming that Nowecki had to use the chemical at issue to perform its dry cleaning service, the problem facing Nowecki was

---

[6] For a more complete discussion of how to identify a client's interests, see ROGER FISHER & WILLIAM L. URY, GETTING TO YES 44–50 (1981); ROY J. LEWICKI, ET AL., NEGOTIATION 116–18 (3rd ed. 1999).

identifying the best choice among the various alternatives for acquiring the chemical.

Nowecki was very interested in a long-term contract for the chemical because it was concerned about recent volatility in the price and it wanted a reliable cost for that critical input into its cleaning process. The chemical price had ranged from $30 to $65 in the previous year. Its current supplier, Northern, did not offer long-term supply contracts, but rather sold the chemical only on demand at the then-current price. Nowecki was interested in a contract of at least three years duration, but was willing to consider a two year deal.

3C offered multi-year contracts of two, three and five years at prices that it would negotiate with each chemical user. The other supplier, Bradley, offered two or four year contracts at a price announced daily on its website. At the time that Nowecki sat down with 3C to discuss a multi-year contract, Bradley was offering a two year contract at $47/pound and a four year contract at $49/pound. Nowecki also had to weigh other concerns, including the advance notice to the supplier required prior to Nowecki receiving the chemical, the amount of time allowed for payment and the supplier's reputation for service. These factors all weighed in favor of its then-current supplier, Northern. Putting all of this information together, Nowecki's alternatives looked something like this:

	Demand Price	Contract Price	Services/Billing
3C	$40	2 year – Negotiable 3 year – Negotiable 5 year – Negotiable	7 day pre-order requirement Good service reputation 30 days to pay
Bradley Supply	$41	2 years - $47 4 years - $49	7 day pre-order requirement Poor service reputation 30 days to pay
Northern Chemical (Current Supplier)	$40	N/A	1 day pre-order requirement Excellent service experience 15 days to pay

Figure 14–1.

Nowecki preferred Bradley's four year contract to the two year deal. Bradley's poor service reputation and worse pre-order and payment terms made negotiating with 3C a better first option.

Determining Nowecki's BATNA in the negotiations with 3C requires comparing the option of sticking with Northern Chemical (and thus foregoing a long-term contract) with the option of signing a 4 year contract with Bradley at $49/pound. If Nowecki prefers Northern's on-demand ordering to a four year deal with Bradley because of concern over service quality, pre-ordering requirements and payment terms, then Nowecki's BATNA entering negotiations with 3C would be its current purchasing arrangement. If Nowecki couldn't arrange a deal with 3C that better met its interests than its then-existing supply arrangement, it would have walked away from the negotiations. Conversely, if Nowecki so highly valued having a long-term contract that it would take Bradley's 4 year deal over continuing purchases from Northern, then the Bradley option is the BATNA to a deal with 3C.

Compared to a reservation price in distributive negotiations, a multi-dimensional BATNA provides a less precise but more flexible and comprehensive yardstick to measure the minimum acceptable deal in the negotiations. In most transaction negotiations and in many litigation matters, the parties will hold more nuanced concerns that are better measured by the broader concept of BATNA than by reservation price alone.

14.2.3 RIGHTS AND RESOURCES

A party preparing well for negotiations knows the resources it can bring to bear in the negotiations. One obvious resource in negotiations involving an attorney is the legal rights possessed by a party under applicable law. In the context of distributive negotiations in litigation, the legal rights of the party usually are defined by the merits evaluation, as set forth in Section 8.2. The legal rights of the party in a potential transaction also can be critical to the resources that will shape that party's approach to the negotiation. Law imposes requirements for or limits on a possible agreement of the parties, or empowers one party with the right to force an outcome in whole or part.[7]

Legal Requirements for/Limits on Agreements. One reason for involving attorneys in negotiations is that they can inform the parties about the legal framework that will constrain the choices of the parties. For example, possible transactions often are shaped by regulatory requirements. The parties may want to build a gas station on a certain site which would require a special zoning variance. Or the buyer of a parcel of land may want to know if it is also assuming pollution remediation liability under environmental laws. Sometimes the law limits a deal not by regulation but rather by creating limits on or presumptions against certain types of agreements. Contract law, for instance, makes certain agreements impermissible, such as an over-reaching non-compete provision in an employment agreement.

Legal Right to Shape or Determine Outcome. Alternatively, a party may possess a legal right that arguably can force an outcome, or at least an outcome on some aspect of the deal. Mr. Bailey may have determined he had the legal right to trim a shrub that sat partly on his property line. Nonetheless, a party with the power to force a resolution has the choice of exercising that power or attempting to create a better resolution by negotiating a different, voluntary outcome with the other party.

Or consider the situation of a professional baseball team that has the right to exercise a contract option extending the player's obligation to the team. The team can exercise the option and pay the player a certain sum for the following season, or it can pay the player a lesser sum if it decides not to extend the contract for the next season. The team has a choice not only between these options, but also whether to engage with the player in negotiating a new contract.

---

[7] As with any aspect of legal representation, the rights and obligations of the parties may be disputable so that the evaluation of legal rights will involve judgments about probabilities of outcomes if litigated.

Of course, not all resources are related to legal rights.[8] A large employer likely will have in-house legal counsel and human relations staff to handle an employment dispute. Legal representation for an individual employee who is not highly compensated may depend on an attorney taking the case on a contingency basis.

14.3   OPTIONS IN CLIENT COUNSELING

In his influential book about practice across numerous professions, Professor Donald Schon describes as follows the situation facing attorneys who take on the responsibility of assisting clients:

> [W]henever anybody comes to a lawyer with a grievance to be redressed or a suit to be pursued, that situation is inherently uncertain. It is uncertain in the sense that it involves first of all what the client says he wants, what he says his interests are. It also involves the lawyer's perception of what the client's interests really are. It involves the issue of how to gauge the prospects for success. It could involve as well the lawyer's sense of the nature of the interactions of interests, power and rights in the larger situation in which this particular matter arises. The lawyer who actually takes all that into account would, I think, say that the client has presented her with a situation of uncertainty, and that her problem is 'how to construct out of this situation a problem she can solve.' If the lawyer doesn't respond in this way, it seems to me that her eventual 'solution' to the client's situation will be Procrustean— it will involve just cutting off whatever doesn't fit.[9]

Counseling a client is the process of taking the client's "inherently uncertain" situation and converting that situation into options for actions that can be taken or authorized by the client. The process of identifying and evaluating options is the focus of this section.

14.3.1   WHAT IS AN "OPTION" IN CLIENT COUNSELING?

You have already encountered two events that would necessarily involve counseling the client about a decision—deciding the amount of an initial settlement offer (or responsive offer), as discussed in Chapter 9; and the decision about reservation price and concession amounts in mediation, as discussed in Chapter 11.   Creating options in client counseling is a

---

[8] For more extensive discussion of various forms of power that can be used by parties in negotiations that are not based on legal rights, see STEFAN H KRIEGER & RICHARD K. NEUMANN, JR., ESSENTIAL LAWYERING SKILLS: INTERVIEWING, COUNSELING, NEGOTIATION, AND PERSUASIVE FACT ANALYSIS 316–22 (4th ed. 2011).

[9] DONALD A. SCHÖN, EDUCATING THE REFLECTIVE PRACTITIONER (1987).

process distinct from asking the client to make these sorts of choices about a matter in the representation.

Imagine an individual client overwhelmed with debt who seeks the assistance of a consumer bankruptcy attorney. Many clients will visit attorneys who present the client a choice that is something like the following: "I will file a bankruptcy for you for $X, which will have the effect of discharging (some or all of) your debts." The client is being asked to make a decision—file for bankruptcy or live with debts. This is the "Procrustean" solution described by Professor Schon.[10]

In many instances, however, the consumer seeking out a bankruptcy attorney is presenting a situation that might involve a range of possible actions, with bankruptcy being one of the most consequential actions on the list. This list of possible actions may include the following:

1. Do nothing.

2. Negotiate with some or all creditors.

3. Default on some debt and attempt to repay other debt (with attention to which debts are "secured" by the debtor's collateral).

4. Enter a debt consolidation and management program.

5. Exercise the debtor's right to stop debt collection harassment.

6. File bankruptcy: (a) under chapter 7 of the Bankruptcy Code, or (b) under chapter 13 of the Bankruptcy Code.

7. Initiate a lawsuit (either individually or as representative plaintiff for a class action) for violations of federal or state consumer protection laws.

Many of these actions are not mutually exclusive. Depending on the circumstances presented by the client, the list of possible actions may be shorter or longer than the above seven items.

The attorney can counsel the client by combining her understanding of the particular client's underlying interests with the available actions to create options for consideration by the client. For instance, the client tells the attorney initially that she just wants her debts to go away with bankruptcy. Upon further exploration, the attorney discovers that she has a car loan that she pays faithfully because she needs her car for her job and she has two debts in default—$12,000 owed to a medical service provider and a $25,000 credit card debt. The attorney further discovers that what motivated her to seek the help of a bankruptcy attorney was

---

[10] This is not to say that such legal service is a bad idea, on the whole. For the reasons discussed in Section 1.5, money dictates to a larger extent the shape of legal services. There are usually strict limits on the amount of money that debt-burdened clients can spend on legal representation. A thorough evaluation of all the option options for each client is not always a viable business model for either the attorney or the client who might pay the legal services bill.

that she cannot sleep at night because of the pressure from the abusive tactics employed by the debt collector who now owns the credit card debt, and that she has had to seek psychiatric help because of the stress from the collector repeatedly improperly threatening to seize her car if she does not pay the credit card debt.

After collecting further information about the financial position and debts of the client, the attorney is able to use her knowledge of bankruptcy and consumer finance law (along with some quick legal research) to identify four possible options for possible actions, as follows:

A. Do nothing.

B. File a chapter 13 bankruptcy.

C. Write the debt collector and demand, under the Fair Debt Collection Practices Act, that the collector cease contact with her, along with attempting to negotiate a loan modification with the mortgage lender.

D. Authorize the attorney to initiate a lawsuit (or threaten to do so in a demand letter) for violations of the Fair Debt Collection Practices Act and seek enough in damages to cover at least the amount of the credit card debt, along with attempting to negotiate a loan modification with the mortgage lender.

The attorney then can describe to the client the possible rewards, risks and costs of each option and the client can decide on a course of action among the options, including initiation of more than one of the actions that are not mutually exclusive.

There is a difference between presenting clients with decisions to be made that require yes/no or fill in the blank answers, and doing this sort of hard work of eliciting the client's motivating interests and shaping possible options that combine an understanding of these client's interests with available actions to meet those interests. Both activities have value. In many situations, attorneys add value and act efficiently by simply answering yes/no questions about their area of the law or assisting clients to resolve a decisive question. Yet the process of option generation and evaluation is the more complex art of client counseling.

14.3.2 GENERATING OPTIONS

It is impossible to provide instruction generally applicable to creating options in client counseling because option generation is dependent on the specific circumstances of each client and the general context of the representation. The process of identifying option generation for a client who has been sexually assaulted at work and seeks protection and redress will differ sharply from a client who wants assistance in structuring a corporate employee benefit program. This section describes two concerns that frequently recur in a variety of legal counseling contexts: (1) identifying the people who will generate options, and (2) techniques for creating value options in integrative negotiation.

People Involved in Option Generation.   Option generation in legal representation can be seen as a process that develops from the attorney to the client to the other side.

> Attorney. Attorneys gain clients and earn fees by creating options for action based on their knowledge of the law. The bankruptcy attorney in the situation described above is able to help the client by offering the potential to file a bankruptcy petition with the court, as well as provide representation in a possible lawsuit for violation of consumer protection laws. The business law attorney who advises a client about organizing a new business entity generates options for the client based on knowledge of the law of incorporation and business formation. Option formation starts with the attorney's application of the law to the problem and facts presented by the client.

> Attorney-Client Collaboration.   Unfortunately, in too many representation matters the attorney ends the process of option generation with a list of possible actions based on the attorney's knowledge of the law.   Attorneys and clients often can collaborate during a counseling session to develop choices based on an exchange of ideas about how to resolve the problem. Attorneys know the law, but clients know their problem and themselves. Clients know what matters to them, what resources are available to them, and the environment in which the dispute or opportunity arises.

> Clients also likely know much about the other party to the transaction or dispute. In distributive negotiations, the attorney aims to form a best estimate about whether a ZOPA exists, and if so, the shape of that ZOPA. This evaluative process requires thinking about how to best estimate the opposing party's reservation price.   Similarly, in preparing for integrative negotiations attorneys search for information about the interests of the other person. Clients often have useful information about how that party will see the matter, and in some cases the client will have intimate knowledge of the other side's concerns and needs. The client counseling session is an opportunity to use this knowledge to brainstorm options for actions to take in the representation.

> Opposing Party Collaboration.   Many integrative negotiation theorists encourage the parties to mutually define the problem presented in the negotiation and then engage in collective

creation of alternative solutions. These theorists often envision an open and trust-building process in which each party shares its interests as part of creating possible acceptable solutions.[11] As cautioned in Section 13.2.1, the distributive issues lurking in almost any legal negotiation requires a thoughtful and cautious approach to this process. Nonetheless, an important insight of the integrative negotiation model is that in proper conditions parties can work together creatively to mutually generate options that can result in an agreement.

Opposing Attorney Collaboration. Finally, negotiating without the presence of the client provides opportunities for exploring options, in addition to the restrictions that come from limited client authority to settle. Attorneys can suggest options not yet approved by the client, with appropriate disclaimer, that test the willingness of the other party to engage in integrative negotiations or that probe the other side's boundaries for compromise. For example, an attorney might state, "My client has made clear that it will not agree to a five year equipment lease at $25,000 per month. I haven't discussed this with the client, but I think it might be willing to consider a three year deal with some substantial reserve for equipment maintenance. Do you think that is possible here?" Suggestions of this sort should be carefully considered as to what it reveals about the client's interests, but it can be a useful way to open topics of discussion without making binding commitments. Just remember that the client may be displeased by having to reject a tentative deal explored by the attorneys, so know well the interests and motivations of the client before proposing options not discussed with the client.

Finding Value-Creating Options. Inventing value-creating options in integrative negotiation is a creative and flexible process. Attorneys can serve clients by bringing the same creativity and openness to the counseling process during which the attorney and client imagine possible options for completing a deal with the other party. Two concepts underlying many successful integrative negotiations are recognizing opportunities to expand the resources available to the negotiators and exploiting differences between the parties' interests and resources.[12]

Expand the Pie. Parties are more likely to find an agreeable solution if the parties can expand the amount of value to be distributed, which reduces the need to distribute a fixed amount. Work with the client in counseling to determine if there is a way

---

[11] *See, e.g.,* ROGER FISHER & WILLIAM L. URY, GETTING TO YES 60–63 (1981).

[12] For a more complete explanation of the process of generating value-creating options, see ROY J. LEWICKI, ET AL., NEGOTIATION 118–24 (3rd ed. 1999).

to re-conceptualize the problem so that there is more value on the table—a bigger pie to slice.

Change the frame of the dispute from the distribution of value as the problem is currently envisioned to increasing future resources. A common tactic for some transactional matters is to think about performance-based compensation. If the transaction helps to make the pie grow, the parties to the transaction have more future value to distribute. This arrangement has the additional benefit of bringing the parties together in mutual benefit from the success of the transaction.

<u>Exploit Complimentary Differences</u>. Attorneys also can work with the client in counseling to find differences in resources or priorities that can be used to create value for both parties. Look for complementary preferences, needs or resources between the parties that can form the basis of a deal.

For example, evaluate the situation facing an accounting firm seeking to sublease half of its space for the five years remaining on its lease. A photography partnership is very interested in the space, but has decided it can afford no more than $2,500 in monthly rent. The accounting firm wants $3,500 per month and has decided that it will attract a tenant willing to pay that rent and thus will not reduce the price, although it thinks the photography firm is a good fit and would like to complete a deal. A partner from the photography business interviews a partner from both businesses about how they operate. These two individuals jointly develop the following three possible options to close the gap based on complementary resources of the accounting firm and the photography partnership:

1. The accounting firm has a full-time receptionist while the part-time receptionist for the photography business recently quit. The photography business could pay for some of the receptionist's time and use the savings from not paying its own receptionist to compensate for the higher rent.

2. The photography firm can bring its accounting business to the accounting firm.

3. The space the photography firm wants to lease has a conference room in which the photographers can meet with clients. The vast majority of its clients like to meet in the late afternoon, evenings or on weekends. The accounting firm sometimes needs a second conference during normal business hours. The photography partnership can offer to share its conference room during morning and early afternoon hours for a decrease in rent.

A thorough examination of the situation facing potential participants in a deal can yield possible alternative solutions based on the differing needs and resources of the parties.

Log-rolling.   Differing priorities between the parties among multiple issues also offers the chance for the attorney to find value through a process known as "log-rolling." [13]   An attorney can suggest to the client accepting a worse outcome on a lower priority issue for the client if the opposing party more highly values an outcome on that issue.   In turn, the opposing party would concede to a position favored by the client on an issue of higher priority to that client.   In the examples of public enforcement actions from section 13.3, if the state environmental agency is vitally concerned about remedying the groundwater problem and less concerned about obtaining a large civil penalty in the case, it can reduce its demand on the civil penalty in exchange for an agreement that the company will promptly conduct specified remediation activities.[14] Log-rolling is a less of a "win-win" solution than a "lose some to get more" situation for both parties.

14.3.3 CLIENT DECISION–MAKING

After the attorney and client have identified available options, the attorney helps the client evaluate the options and make a decision about how to proceed. Section 11.2.1 sets forth some guiding principles when counseling clients to arrive at decision about reservation price, including the following: manage client expectations, involve the client in the evaluative process, lead the client to client to take responsibility for and ownership over the final decision. All of these principles apply to counseling clients in transaction matters and prior to negotiations with multiple options and issues. This section builds on those principles by examining two circumstances that attorneys regularly confront in client counseling—delivering bad news and counseling irrational clients.

Unwelcome Advice: Bad News.   Part of evaluating options is the unenviable task in some cases of explaining to the client that the option it most prefers is not legally viable or carries substantial legal risks. A divorcing spouse who wants full custody of children does not want to hear that the court is highly unlikely to provide this outcome. Effectively delivering bad news is a skill worth learning.

---

[13] "Log-rolling" is a term that arose from observation of legislators trading votes on one bill for votes on another bill. For example, Senator R from Nevada agrees to vote for building a bridge in Kentucky if Senator M from Kentucky agrees to vote for saving a military base in Nevada.

[14] Negotiating scholars have given little attention to this dynamic in negotiating, but for a theoretical (and, again, mathematical-oriented) treatment of the issue, *see* http://ieeexplore. ieee.org/stamp/stamp.jsp?tp=&arnumber=1173685.

Law professor and professional mediator Marjorie Corman emphasizes two strategies for delivering bad news to legal clients. First, don't be overly blunt, but don't stall.[15] It is obviously ill-advised to start a counseling session with a spouse who seeks full custody he will not obtain by saying, "I want to let you know that there is virtually no chance that you will be awarded full custody of the children." Yet it is little better to review the dissolution court process, discuss maintenance payments and then get around to the bad news at the end of the meeting. Professor Corman summarizes her experience with this latter tactic as resulting in clients "feeling as if the lawyer had heartlessly walked them to the edge of the cliff and dropped them over the side."[16]

Research suggests legal clients, like medical patients, react best when the bad news is the lead topic of the discussion but it is prefaced by a brief showing of empathy for the client's position and a brief preparation that the attorney is going to be providing unwelcome advice. In some cases, Professor Corman suggests, it may be appropriate to lead with an inquiry about the client's expectations on the issue. For instance, asking a client who has recently sent the attorney incriminating documents to produce to the other side, "Did the documents you sent to our office last week cause you any concerns about the case?" The client's answer may lead to an opening to discuss the likelihood of losing on a motion before the court.

Second, "be direct and scrupulously accurate."[17] The attorney should be prepared to explain in detail exactly how he reached the conclusion that the client does not want to hear. Resist the temptation to "soft pedal" bad news, which can lead the client to believe that the preferred outcome is still possible or likely. Consider explaining the reasoning in support of the conclusion in a way that emphasizes the attorney's advocacy for the client. After the prefatory remarks and having delivering the bad news punch line, start with an explanation of the client's position, including the attorney's efforts to find support for that position in the law. After demonstrating understanding of the client's perspective and the attorney's advocacy for the client, explain why the law does not support that position.[18]

Part of an accurate explanation is being precise about the advice that the attorney is providing. An attorney who has concluded that the client only has a small chance (perhaps 15% for those who like to quantify) to obtain a desired zoning variance for a proposed office development may tell the client, "after looking closely at this matter, it just does not seem possible

---

[15] MARJORIE CORMAN AARON, CLIENT SCIENCE: ADVICE FOR LAWYERS ON COUNSELING CLIENTS THROUGH BAD NEWS AND OTHER LEGAL REALITIES 12–19 (2012).

[16] *Id.* at 17

[17] *Id.* at 14

[18] Professor Corman recommends that an attorney in litigation employ a three step process: forcefully make the argument for the client that the attorney would make to the court, make the other side's argument, and then explain why the other side is likely to prevail. *Id.* at 24.

that we can get you the variance you will need to build an office building on that site." This would be an inaccurate legal conclusion to convey. The client needs to hear that is "highly unlikely," "very long odds," "a roughly 15% chance" or the like, not that it is impossible. The client may be a risk-taker, or it may have reasons for viewing a failure to obtain a permit as an acceptable loss.

Irrational Clients. A realtor sells to one of his clients a house owned by Z Enterprises. The realtor is the principal owner of Z Enterprises, but he does not disclose his ownership in Z Enterprises to the homebuyer, which is a clear breach of the realtor's fiduciary duty to the homebuyer. The homebuyer learns about the conflict and informs the state licensing authority of the situation. The state licensing authority tells the realtor's attorney that it will close the investigation without a discipline action if the realtor agrees to take extra training courses on the duties of a real estate agent. The realtor's attorney strongly recommends to the realtor that he accept this offer because the licensing authority could have sought to have his realtor's license revoked and almost certainly would obtain a finding that the realtor breached his fiduciary duty. The realtor responds to his attorney, "no deal!—I will stand on my principles because I don't think it is fair to punish me for selling a good house."

What should the attorney do with this demonstrably irrational client? Definitely reiterate and verify, but otherwise there is little that an attorney can do in this situation.[19] The client may be making a terrible decision, but it is the client's decision to make. Attorneys faced with this sort of situation probably should make extra efforts to make exceedingly clear to the client all the reasons for the attorney's contrary advise and all of the foreseeable consequences of the client's decision, then verify the client wants to proceed with the ill-advised choice.[20]

---

[19] Of course, the attorney does not have to accept client decisions that would violate the attorney's ethical requirements. For instance, if the realtor responded that he not only is rejecting the licensing authority's offer but also wants the attorney to sue the licensing authority for defamation for making the offer, the attorney has an obligation not to file such a frivolous suit. In any case, the attorney always has the option of discontinuing the attorney-client relationship when doing so is ethically permissible.

[20] The attorney also would be advised to document this action with a letter to the client or at least a memo to the file. If the realtor later sues the attorney for malpractice when the realtor loses his license, this type of document would make quick work of that claim.